# closing the gap

### SECOND EDITION

a revolutionary approach to client
and donor services

∽

## Scott Farnsworth, JD, CFP©

∽

**SUNBRIDGE**

SunBridge Publishing
Harmony, Florida

SUNBRIDGE

Published by SunBridge Publishing, a division of SunBridge, Inc.

Visit our website at www.SunBridgeNetwork.com

The SunBridge logo is a trademark of SunBridge, Inc.

Farnsworth, Scott
Closing the Gap: (Second Edition) A Revolutionary Approach to Client and Donor
Services / Scott Farnsworth
ISBN 978-0-9839595-0-2

Cover and book design by Julie Hoyt Dorman, jdorman@branchhill.net

Printed in the United States of America

For information about purchasing this book for business or promotional use, or for special sales and quantity discounts, please contact SunBridge Publishing: admin@SunBridgeNetwork.com

# contents

# acknowledgements

> *"If I have seen further than other men,*
> *it is because I have stood on the shoulders of giants."*
> —*Sir Isaac Newton*

Unlike Sir Isaac Newton, I do not claim to have seen further than other men and women; but like him, I have stood on the shoulders of giants. Some of the sturdiest of those shoulders belong to the hundreds of financial advisors, estate planning attorneys, and philanthropic professionals who have taken SunBridge training and are living its principles each day.

It takes a bit of courage to try something new and let go of old ways of doing things. In addition, it requires love of a better path, and willingness to walk it. Each of them brought these laudable qualities and more to our work together, and each of them has benefited, professionally and personally, as a result. I acknowledge each of these fine individuals and thank them for their faith in SunBridge and in this approach.

These visionary pilgrims have been my partners and collaborators in this marvelous journey into the frontier. They have played an indispensable role in blazing a new trail to a truly client- or donor-centered model of practice, where the advisor meets the client or donor at whatever level the client or donor may be, and then invites the client or donor to move—at the client's or donor's pace—to increasingly more profound levels of advisor/client relationship.

Ultimately, at Level Three, the professional advisor serves clients or donors as an architect of sorts, helping them define and design a future of greater abundance, purpose, and significance; as the drafter of the blueprints of that envisioned future; and then as a general contractor in turning their blueprint into reality.

These pioneers have been able to see a future for themselves of working with their clients or donors in this way, and in turn, are enjoying greater abundance, purpose, and significance in their own lives. I honor the vision, courage, compassion, and loyalty of these phenomenal men and women, and thank them on behalf of the many future generations of SunBridge advisors and their clients and donors who will benefit in following the trail they have blazed.

I am deeply indebted to Sharon Greenway and Cyndi Campbell who presently work with me at SunBridge, and others, including Debbie Warner and Rosemary Ghezzi, who have done so in the past. Their diligence, loyalty, creativity, and commitment have been an indispensible part of the progress we have made in bringing this vision to reality.

Finally, I acknowledge that I do not have the language to adequately express my gratitude and appreciation to my most brilliant, insightful, and trustworthy counselor, my wife and eternal soul mate, Marcie. She and I began a quest 36 years ago to forge a family that can be together forever. We deeply love our six children, Elisabeth, Nathaniel, Sara, Kate, Evan, and Paul, and our six grandchildren, Henry, Sophie, Walker, Eli, Daisy, and Penny. These thirteen people represent the greatest abundance, purpose, and significance in my life.

Scott Farnsworth,
President
SunBridge, Inc.
3214 Bayflower Avenue
Harmony, Florida 34773
407-593-2386
scott@SunBridgeNetwork.com
*www.SunBridgeNetwork.com*

# foreword

B oth of us have enjoyed long, successful, and rewarding careers, Mike as a financial consultant, non-profit executive, and philanthropic advisor, and Mary as the head of the Disney Institute and then as an executive, family, and business coach. We have each worked to be on the cutting edge of developments within our respective specialties, seeking to provide our clients the best possible service.

All along, we've held convictions that there was "a better way to do things" when it comes to helping clients and families plan for their futures. Unfortunately, our sense was that this ideal wasn't fully addressed and delivered in the way most professionals work with their clients and families.

Life sometimes offers us serendipitous moments, such as when there suddenly appears another who shares that same vision, that same quest to deliver deeper, richer, and more meaningful service to clients and families. That is what happened when we each met Scott. We found we shared a passion for working with people—not merely their money and their property—but living, breathing, always fascinating human beings living real lives in real families. We also found that his groundbreaking work at SunBridge was often a catalyst for pushing our ideas forward

Over time, our long-standing relationship and our shared vision and passion developed into a full partnership for serving affluent families. In this "new paradigm for successful families," as we call it, we offer to meet people where they are and then extend to them a continuum of services ranging from hard-core number crunching and tax savings to implementing the grandest vision they can imagine for the next 100 years for their family. We have found immense satisfaction and rich rewards in this work.

The insights, principles, processes, and tools Scott shares in this book are key elements of our success in working together. Our clients thrive on working with advisors who love them and who focus first on understanding them and their hopes, fears, dreams, perspectives, and challenges, rather than on our possible solutions. They appreciate that we are committed to walking alongside them as trusted friends, each bringing our individual expertise, experiences, and skills to the table to serve them.

The joyful journey that is our Legacy Planning Associates business is based on seeing our client families as whole people in need of holistic solutions, and as fellow experts and collaborators. The lessons in this book are guideposts and milestones for those who wish to create a similar approach for their work with clients and donors. They may discover, as we have, that touching hearts, connecting families, and changing lives—perhaps for generations to come—is holy and inspired work indeed.

We invite you to share the passion and the extraordinary fulfillment of this work. It's not for the lazy or the faint of heart, but then, nothing of lasting value ever is.

Mike Cummins and Mary Tomlinson
Principals, Legacy Planning Associates, LLC
*www.LegacyPlans.com*
Orlando, Florida

# closing the gap

SECOND EDITION

a revolutionary approach to client
and donor services

∽

dedicated to

## Marcie Hobbs Farnsworth

brilliant – beautiful – spiritual – wise – kind

∽

# preface

Anais Nïn wrote, "We see the world not as it is, but as we are." This holds true in our professional dealings just as much as in our social and personal life. The aim of this book, which provides a revolutionary approach to client and donor service for financial advisors, estate planners, and philanthropic professionals based on the SunBridge model, is to expand your vision of what constitutes professional advisory services. This in turn will naturally expand the world of your work, its value to your clients and donors, and your sense of significance and purpose both professionally and personally.

All of this may seem like a grand promise, and it is—but it is a promise I see fulfilled every day. The approach and tools offered in the pages that follow will not just change your practice; they'll change you. Many of your colleagues around the world who have been trained in the SunBridge method have come to feel that their work life has taken on a new dimension and depth. I believe you'll feel the same. By contrast, the traditional way of doing business may seem flat, linear; a presentation in black-and-white instead of living color.

The foundation of this approach is an ancient idea, and the essence of simplicity: By bringing an experience of value, significance, meaning, purpose, and fulfillment to your clients and donors, you'll create an environment in which you receive the same. The main reasons we financial advisors, estate planners, and philanthropic professionals have been unable to put this principle into practice are that, first, we haven't had the standard that would allow us to see that we were falling far short of it, and second, we haven't had the tools that would give us a way to translate such a standard into practice. *Closing the Gap* provides both.

There is an old Hindu parable about six blind men who are asked by a person with sight to describe an elephant standing beside them. One blind man feels the elephant's trunk, and says, "It is like a great snake." The second puts his hand against the creature's side, and says, "No, it is like a wall." The third man feels the elephant's leg, and reports, "Not at all; this animal is like a mighty tree." The fourth blind man, feeling the elephant's tusk, says, "You're all wrong. This animal is like a spear." The fifth and sixth men feel the elephant's ear and tail, respectively, and begin arguing: "This beast is like a fan!" "No, it is like a rope." And this goes on.

Though each man is partly right, all are in the wrong—not because of what they have envisioned, but because of what they have failed to take into account from the reports of the others. In much the same way, traditional financial advising addresses only a small part of the reality of client and donor service, ignoring the rest, and "missing the elephant" standing right before it.

As you will soon see, this deficiency of traditional professional advising which keeps it from seeing the big picture is based on reducing client and donor service to a transaction-based activity centered around money. Such activity, while undeniably part of the "elephant," is just one part. Money actually is not the most important form of a client's wealth, but we professionals have trained clients and donors to believe it is, to the point that they don't think of their wealth as something beyond money and property, and don't even realize that they can and should be asking us questions of value and meaning that go beyond this.

I firmly believe that professional advisors who do not rise to the challenge of meeting the needs of their clients and donors as human beings, who do not shift beyond the old transaction-based approach to client and donor service, will have increasing difficulty succeeding and even surviving professionally in the years just ahead.

For reasons that will become clear along the way, we're going to begin with a metaphor—one involving an unusual place called "Flatland," and its inhabitants. Like many metaphors, this one has the power to inspire new vision, spark change, and set us on a journey. As you make this journey that begins in Flatland and eventually leads to the rich and rewarding practice of client and donor service in an expanding universe of meaning and purpose, know that our best wishes go with you every step of the way.

# SECTION 1

# client service in flatland: level one

*"Either you will develop a
significant relationship with your clients
or your competitors will."*

—Samuel J. Taylor, Certified Investment Management Analyst

In 1884, Edwin A. Abbott, an English clergyman, Shakespearian scholar, and author wrote what has become a timeless piece of satire on science and mathematics, called *Flatland: A Romance of Many Dimensions*. In this book, Abbott introduces us to an imaginary, two-dimensional world with width and breadth, but no depth, a world he calls "Flatland."

We may think of Flatland as a geometric plane. One of the observations Abbott makes about such a world is that its inhabitant would not experience anything like what we experience as objects, not even two-dimensional ones. The reason for this is that in order to perceive two-dimensional shapes such as circles or squares, the perceiver has to be in a different plane relative to them—he has to be in what Abbott calls "Spaceland." For Flatlanders, circles, squares and other geometric shapes would appear only as lines, since they would have to be perceived from the side, as it were. From Abbott's book:

> Place a penny on the middle of one of your tables in Space; and leaning over it, look down upon it. It will appear a circle.

> But now, drawing back to the edge of the table, gradually lower your eye (thus bringing yourself more and more into the condition of the inhabitants of Flatland), and you will find the penny becoming more and more oval to your view, and at last when you have placed your eye exactly on the edge of the table (so that you are, as it were, actually a Flatlander) the penny will then have ceased to appear oval at all, and will have become, so far as you can see, a straight line.

> The same thing would happen if you were to treat in the same way a Triangle, or a Square, or any other figure cut out from pasteboard. As soon as you look at it with your eye on the edge of the table, you will find that it ceases to appear to you as a figure, and that it becomes in appearance a straight line.

> **Some clients and donors recognize the relative superficiality of traditional professional services, and imagine a world having more than two dimensions.**

In Flatland, everything appears as no more than a line, including relationships between people, who relate to each other literally with no depth. The superficiality of interactions is not a problem in Flatland; the inhabitants, having no standard for comparison, take it for granted. They see each other in the simplest terms: as approaching or receding, more or less angular, and so on.

Now, I ask you to consider the following claim, which it will be the aim of the rest of this book to clarify and substantiate: Professional advisors who offer traditional client and donor service unwittingly create and perpetuate a kind of Flatland in which both they and their clients or donors are often trapped. Within this one-dimensional reality, which in the SunBridge model is called "Level One," the various services that the advisor delivers seem complete to the client or donor, just as any Flatlander would regard the linear reality in which he lives (if he gave it any thought at all) as complete.

But it is far from it. As with all lines, the relationship between the Level-One advisor and the client or donor is described by two points: the client's need for certain financial, legal or philanthropic products or services and the advisor's knowledge of how to deliver them. In a typical Level-One transaction, Mr. Jones goes to see Ms. Lane, a financial planner, to try to get a better return on his investment. After examining a number of options, Ms. Lane recommends a tax-deferred variable annuity or some other financial product, completes the required application, invests the client's money, and delivers the executed documents.

In the case of an estate planning transaction, Mr. Jones might go to see Mr. Smith, an estate planner, because he realizes he needs a will. Mr. Smith asks him a list of questions about his material assets, the natural objects of his bounty, and perhaps his interest in charitable giving. Mr. Smith then prepares the necessary documents, reviews them with the client, oversees their execution, and delivers a large stack of paper to Mr. Jones, perhaps in a fancy binder.

In the world of philanthropy, Ms. Wilson, a fundraising professional from a well-regarded nonprofit, may approach Mr. Jones, who has supported the nonprofit in its previous campaigns. She explains how his contributions will further the nonprofit's mission and recommends the size of gift she thinks he might be willing to consider during this round of giving. Mr. Jones thinks about it for a few days, agrees to make the gift and writes the check.

These transactions, which are fairly typical, may sound complete to you, and they are as far as they go. For nearly twenty years, I certainly regarded them as complete, until the day a suspicious client jolted me out of my Flatland view of the world.

About fifteen years ago, I had a highly successful Level-One practice as an estate planning attorney and private trustee in a small town in the South. I was a sole practitioner with an excellent staff of four full-time personal assistants. I owned my own office building and enjoyed a reputation as an excellent lawyer and a thoughtful, considerate, and honest person. My CPA told me he believed I was the highest-paid attorney in town, and perhaps best of all, I took off 165 days a year from the practice.

One day, I was reviewing with some clients a set of estate planning documents I had prepared for them. They studied them carefully as we worked our way through them, and then on about page 27, the husband stopped me. "Mr. Farnsworth," he said. (I've since learned that whenever someone twice your age calls you "Mister," you're probably in trouble. I was.)

"When we first sat down with you a few days ago, we had a wonderful conversation about us, about our children and grandchildren, about our faith and the values that make our family what it is today and what we hope it will become in the future. It seemed to us that you understood all of that at the time. But now that we're looking at these documents, we don't see any of that in here. To be completely honest with you, Mr. Farnsworth, it looks as though you've just plugged our names into one of your forms."

He was right. I had. With the truth out in plain sight, I felt the need to do a little tap-dancing to reassure him; but the truth is the truth, and no amount of tap-dancing, however skillful, changes it. The client accepted my rationale for the moment, but his comment had struck a nerve. In my heart, I knew that this was really all I was doing for my clients, and for the first time, thanks to my client's honesty, I began to realize that this was no longer enough.

I'd been doing what is typical in my profession, and more than adequate by accepted standards, but I came to see that there's a huge gap between what client and donor service typically provides and what it *could* provide—a gap that neither advisor nor client may realize exists, but one that leaves them both deeply unfulfilled. In SunBridge, we call this chasm between what is routinely offered to clients and what could be offered, the "Client Service Gap."

# the client service gap

While most advisors and many clients and donors are unwittingly trapped in the linear world of Flatland, thankfully not all of them are. Some clients and donors, like the ones I just mentioned, are beginning to recognize the relative superficiality of traditional financial, philanthropic, and legal services, and are beginning to imagine a world of client services having more than two dimensions.

Many of these clients and donors are members of the baby boomer and later generations. They've had the time and the means to think about the meaning of their lives, rather than being in survival mode like the Depression generation. They often sense a desire to approach financial planning, estate planning, and philanthropic planning as a way to add greater meaning and purpose to their lives, and as a means to affect the lives and causes they deeply care about.

When we asked these clients and donors what sort of services they would like to receive from professional advisors if they could, in contrast with the services they actually do usually receive, this is what we found:

---

**What Clients and Donors Want Most**

Connection • Significance • Vision • Wisdom • Trust

**What Advisors Typically Offer**

Transactions • Numbers • Techniques • Information • Advice

---

The text in the bottom part of the illustration describes the main points that occur along the line of Level-One client and donor service, which is, at least at this stage of the legal, philanthropic, and financial services industries, what most professionals offer. The text along the top identifies what clients and donors consistently say they would like in a relationship with a professional advisor, but believe they're unlikely to find. Remember that clients and donors for the most part have accepted life in Flatland dictated by the industry. They don't know what they don't know, and they don't know they can ask for a different kind of relationship.

The Client Service Gap isn't just a disparity between theory and practice. It's paradigmatic, arising out of two completely different approaches to the client or donor relationship. Once again, it is the old story of the blind men and the elephant, each perceiving a bit of the truth but largely missing the whole picture. Each one's perception, in turn, determines how he or she sees the relationship.

In order to appreciate just how different they are, and the impact that choosing one or the other will have on your practice, let's take a closer look at the key elements that appear in the Client Service Gap illustration.

[
**Beyond the consequences for the client or donor imposed by the Client Service Gap, there are serious side effects for the advisor.**
]

**What Advisors Typically Offer:**

**Transactions** – Formulaic interactions based on financial products and services, documents, legal requirements, and the strictly technical skills of the advisor.

**Numbers** – Quantitative information usually directly related to the client's wealth measured exclusively in terms of money and property. This equates the client to a "balance sheet." "You are what you own."

**Techniques** – The advisor's ability to use his or her special training to translate the client's or donor's needs and wants into financial or legal products and services or forms of giving.

**Information** – The financial facts of the client's or donor's situation, and their financial, philanthropic, and legal world in general. Usually this takes the form of numbers and discussion about the impact of technical requirements (*e.g.,* of law).

**Advice** – Direction the advisor gives the client or donor to solve a legal, financial or philanthropic problem or accomplish a specific financial goal.

**What Clients and Donors Want Most:**

**Connection** – Signifies an ongoing relationship based on intimate knowledge and understanding, developing into a deep and lasting friendship.

**Significance** – A sense of what matters most to the client or donor, a grasp of him or her as a human being whose life has meaning and purpose. A profound understanding of the client's or donor's life and experiences.

**Vision** – A far-reaching sense of what the client's or donor's life can be, and even wants to be. This may span generations in a family, family business, etc.

**Wisdom** – The ability to know what matters and what doesn't; to apply this knowledge by helping clients and donors see the significance of their lives, and unlock their potential to live more richly and fully in every sense.

**Trust** – Confidence that the advisor truly understands the client or donor and what matters most to him or her, and is deeply committed to putting the client's or donor's long-term well-being and fulfillment ahead of the advisor's.

Beyond the consequences for the client or donor imposed by the Client Service Gap, there are serious side effects for the advisor—side effects that fairly compel us to ask new questions and, eventually, to move into a reality with options for greater depth. Some of the more serious effects for the advisor are:

1) The products and services that the advisor sells are largely indistinguishable from those sold by competitors (except perhaps on the basis of price), making positioning all but impossible. As a result, these products and services—and by association, advisors themselves—become commoditized. This drives down value and price, making it necessary for the advisor to offset shrinking profit margins by constantly increasing the number of sales just to maintain the same level of income, which creates a marketing reality of diminishing returns.

2) Because there really is no deep and engaging relationship with the client, eventually, the advisor becomes bored with the repetitive, "cookie cutter" quality of the services he or she provides. No client or donor is going to be more enthusiastic about working with you

than you are about working with them. This is why so many financial professionals experience burnout after even a relatively few number of years in practice.

**3)**   The stability of the advisor's practice remains highly susceptible to shifting economic, legislative, and market conditions. Because the practice is predicated on numbers alone, any changes in laws, regulations, national or world economic conditions, or other factors that affect the numbers, will directly—and often adversely—affect the practice. The unpredictability of such an arrangement fosters in the advisor a sense of anxiety about the future that aggravates the already unsettling marketing reality.

**4)**   A schism develops between the advisor's work and personal life that greatly reduces his or her ability to be useful to clients and donors. While many things may have great relevance and meaning to the advisor personally, there exists no conduit for incorporating these into the professional practice. The sense of work as something fundamentally separate from life increases, with corresponding increases in tedium, indifference, and suspicions of irrelevance apart from dollar values alone. And ultimately, dollar values alone cannot provide any deep or lasting job satisfaction or feeling of usefulness and purpose.

Even financially successful advisors are starting to question the stress, tenuousness, and dearth of personal fulfillment inherent in perpetuating a practice limited to Level-One client service. For example, Mark is an estate planner in a large southwestern city who has a steady stream of clients and a lucrative business; but he's grown bored with the repetitive nature of his practice and alarmed about the effects of Congressional tampering with the estate tax laws and the threat that they'll be eliminated altogether.

"Work just isn't fun anymore," he confided in me. "I didn't get into this profession to become a mechanic, but that's what it feels like a lot of the time." Staying at Level One is a formula for boredom and burnout, one that leads to the advisor getting stuck on what we in SunBridge call "the marketing merry-go-round." The advisor has to keep pushing new people into the pipeline as clients and donors move quickly in and out of the professional relationship.

# level-one client and donor service

I've claimed that Level One client service can be severely limited in its ability to fulfill clients' highest expectations of their professional advisors. What makes Level One so limited? The limitations are inherent in its method, its main focus, its view of the client or donor, and its vision, which are:

- **Method:** Analytical
- **Main Focus:** Money
- **View of Client/Donor:** Balance Sheet
- **Vision:** Quick-Fixes

At Level One, the financial, legal, or philanthropic professional is involved in a primarily analytical process. At the end of this process, he or she will advise the client or donor in the management of money and property, and translate this advice into financial, legal, or philanthropic products or services.

This approach follows the old model of the priesthoods of ancient Greece, India, and others. In these cultures now long past, priests were specialists who served as intermediaries between ordinary people and the divine. Having been highly trained and initiated into the mysteries, they acted as proxies for the uninitiated, and functioned in ways that were unavailable to the hoi polloi. Often, they spoke an arcane language that lay people could not understand.

In a similar way, traditional financial and estate planners and planned giving experts have created and sustained a view of themselves as specialists, initiates in a world of numbers, terms, and rules that the layman typically finds baffling. The value of the consultant, in these terms, lies in his or her ability to guide the client through this mysterious world with the aim of providing quick-fixes for problems directly tied to management of the client's or donor's material assets.

[
**Level-One skills are incorporated,
not rejected, at Level Two.**
]

## Analytical

*"Too much logic bores. Life eludes logic, and everything that
logic alone constructs remains artificial and forced."*
*—André Gide*

Level-One client and donor service is a mental method—linear, logical, and
analytical. When we talk about the mind, or mental processes, we're generally
referring to what's been termed "left-brain" thinking. (Right-brain thinking, which
is creative, intuitive, and holistic, is more often associated with the heart—and
we'll have more to say about this in the next Section.) The left brain can solve
problems, apply rules, and infer conclusions. Clients, however, are much more
than this sort of thinking can grasp, let alone serve. The client, the client's wealth,
the client's life do not exist just analytically. They have a context, significance,
and a living meaning that the logical mind alone cannot fully comprehend.

## Money

*"And you prate the wealth of nations, as if it were bought and
sold, The wealth of nations is men, not silk and cotton and gold."*
*—Richard Hovey*

Service at Level One is based on the assumption that wealth consists of
nothing more than a client's material assets. In the strictly quantitative world of

traditional financial, legal, and philanthropic advising, this has been true; exactly as it is true that in Flatland, everything is a line. The moment we acknowledge that our wealth as humans encompasses much more than our money and property, doors begin to fly open, and client service demands redefinition.

## Balance Sheet

*"My life has more relevance than simple economics after a lifetime of living and contribution. I refuse to be thought of as a balance sheet." —Dr. Barrie Sanford Greiff*

When Level-One advisors get together with their professional colleagues, they tend to talk about their clients and donors as numbers. ("I'm working on a $10 million case," or "Today I'm seeing a potential $50,000 gift.") When clients and donors are seen as numbers, especially as the numbers that measure their net worth, their taxable estate, their investable assets, or their gift-giving capacity, we lose sight of their humanity, the richness of their lives, and the depths of their concerns. They become to us, in a very real way, flat and one-dimensional.

One tragedy of seeing our donors and clients as a number is that we fail to notice how much more we could be providing them, and how much more they could be providing us in return. Wearing number-focused blinders, we blind ourselves to a whole new world of possibilities and we cheat ourselves out of grand opportunities, both personal and professional. Once we take off those blinders and open our eyes to their wholeness, a brilliant new world comes into view.

## Quick-Fixes

*"If the only tool you have is a hammer, you will see every problem as a nail." —Abraham Maslow*

The problem with the quick-fix transaction, as with the other elements of Level One, is that it ignores most of the person. There are issues of meaning, values, vision, significance, wisdom, and purpose that run in deep currents through every life. These forces call out constantly for recognition, respect, expression, and survival. They are alive, and they grow and change as the individual of whom they are such an essential part grows and changes, unfolding over time. Identifying them, then working with them in the context of a financial, estate, or philanthropic plan, requires *discernment*—something we'll examine at length in Section 3 of this book.

These defining elements of Level-One client service actually preclude adding the kind of value that makes possible a long-term, increasingly useful relationship with the client or donor.

# marketing at level one

The traditional, linear form of client and donor service we have been discussing is on the decline. Financial advisors, estate planners, and philanthropic professionals have found themselves dealing with a generation of consumers who have come of age, have more material wealth than ever before, and bring higher expectations than any preceding generation that the key advisors in their life will be men and women with insight, awareness, and compatible values.

As a result, advisors who still practice at Level One are coming to realize that they have to, as Lewis Carroll put it, "run twice as fast as they can just to stay in the same place" when it comes to marketing. They have to continually bring in new business; but as long as this new business focuses on quick-fixes and transactions, every sale or every donation essentially means they will have to start over tomorrow.

At Level One, it's difficult even to imagine ways to add value, but without added value, the relationship with the client remains little more than an isolated, hit-and-run encounter. Further, the clients of Level-One financial advisors often put off long-term, whole-life planning, which leaves the advisor in the unenviable position of having to persuade the client to make a commitment to

> [
> **When it comes to marketing, advisors who still practice at Level One have to "run twice as fast as they can just to stay in the same place."**
> ]

financial services he or she needs. And when the market declines sharply, as it did several times in the last few years, there's a lot of blame and finger-pointing, and eventually shuffling of accounts. With no reservoir of goodwill based on deep relationships, that's not surprising.

For estate planners, it's even worse, because the Level-One service they provide usually centers on death and disability—issues that people routinely put off until, for whatever reason, they can't postpone them any longer. As a result, the Level-One estate planner is constantly working uphill. He or she has no context for answering the question, "What do you talk about with clients after you've covered taxes, death, and disability?" And what do you talk about in the first place when there are few tax issues to consider, as is the case for most clients today? Not surprisingly, a substantial number of estate plans are never signed, even by clients who have already paid for them.

In the case of philanthropic professionals, working at Level One is a shallow game of hide and seek, a frustrating chase that has become increasingly difficult in a world when every prospective donor can screen his or her calls, emails, and texts, and who ignores every direct-mail piece the nonprofit sends. There is a constantly growing need for more giving, and sharply increased pressure from the organization to raise more money, but a diminishing pool of accessible donors to respond to the fund-raisers' pleas. Over time, even those few who will listen tune out or die off. It can be a dreary prospect, pushing the philanthropic professional to move on to yet another nonprofit in search of greener pastures. Unfortunately, there is usually no more grass in the new place than there was in the old.

[
**When clients and donors are seen as numbers,
we lose sight of their humanity. They become to us,
in a very real way, flat and one-dimensional.**
]

# life after level one

Fortunately, there is life after Level One. We aren't sentenced to Flatland forever. Thoughtful reflection on the Client Service Gap suggests three approaches or levels to client service:

**Level One:** the linear, Flatland approach.

**Level Two:** a three-dimensional, far more substantial approach in which the advisor and client can begin to discover and interact with each other as human beings.

**Level Three:** a new approach that lays the groundwork for an organic, long-term, deeply gratifying professional relationship based on the client's or donor's vision of his or her life, and the professional advisor's ability to function as a facilitator and translator of that vision into action steps.

Client service beyond Level One allows you to build your practice so it's successful in *all* ways, with far less time spent marketing than is needed to market a Level-One practice. Referrals and repeat business will become commonplace. Most importantly, you'll see your relationships with your clients transformed from repetitive, short-term transactions to a deeply rewarding, long-term discovery of meaning, significance, and purpose that will enrich you both, in every sense. When you begin working beyond Level One, you'll set into motion the accomplishment of five key goals:

# five goals of practice beyond level one

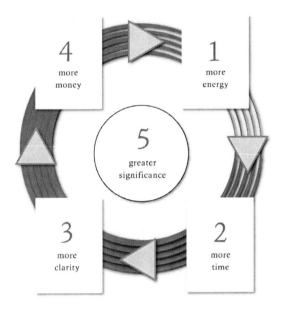

Amazingly, these five goals practically fulfill themselves once the advisor begins to listen and respond to clients and donors as human beings. To accomplish this, the traditional, Level-One practice must undergo a shift from a linear approach toward a more three-dimensional one based on understanding and appreciating the client's or donor's core values, and *seeing wealth as something more than money and property alone*. It must move beyond left-brain, transactional thinking to a more encompassing vision. And it must forsake quick-fixes in favor of a partnership in which the advisor stands ready and able to provide essential service and indispensable value to the client or donor for a lifetime.

In the next section, we leave Flatland behind for the three-dimensional world of Level Two. It may surprise you to learn that this profound advance on Level One is rooted in the oldest form of creative expression we know: the art of storytelling.

# S E C T I O N    2

# escape from flatland: level two

*"There is no agony like bearing an
untold story inside of you."*

—*Maya Angelou*

The Level-Two advisor makes the proverbial quantum leap out of Flatland in a way that inaugurates an entirely different sort of client or donor relationship. Level-Two service adds a new dimension—one in which the human reality of the client or donor supersedes naked numbers on a balance sheet.

In other words, Level-Two advising adds depth. The professional relationship is no longer imprisoned in the monotonous and premeditated conversations dictated by money, products, and services. Something else drives it. The result of this dramatic transformation is that the professional relationship takes on a vitality and usefulness that Level-One service cannot even imagine, let alone offer.

It should be pointed out that, even as our practice starts to evolve into Level Two, many clients and donors will come seeking no more than Level-One products and services. After all, this is what we as a profession have conditioned them to expect from us. Some will never want anything else, even if it's offered, and there's nothing wrong with that. The aim of the SunBridge method is to meet clients and donors where they are, explain the possibility of working at a higher level, invite them to go there if that's what they choose, and then serve them at the level at which they feel comfortable.

But while some clients and donors may not recognize or understand the limitations of the Flatland world in which most of us have spent our professional lives, it's imperative that *we* do. If we fail to do so, our client or donor services and relationships will be imprisoned in Flatland, and we will end up denying ourselves and our clients and donors the opportunity to choose a richer and more rewarding experience.

One of the premises of this book is that both professional advisors and their clients and donors, once introduced to the possibility of working together in a three-dimensional world—and perhaps in an even larger world where the future is envisioned, designed, and constructed according to the most significant issues in the client's or donor's life—can now both make a deliberate and informed choice about whether to stay in Flatland or to move on to more.

Such a choice is feasible only if the advisor *is aware* that it is possible, *can articulate* the options to clients and donors, and then *can deliver* a larger, deeper, richer quality of service.

True choice is not possible unless the professional advisor first becomes mindful of the potential of moving beyond the Flatland world of Level One. The advisor must be able to envision a multidimensional world of professional services.

> It's a shallow game of hide and seek, a frustrating chase when prospective donors screen their calls. Over time, even those who few who will listen tune out or die off.

Next, the professional advisor must learn to communicate that multidimensional vision to others, so that they see clearly what the advisor sees and they understand what the advisor understands. The advisor must become proficient at explaining, comparing, and contrasting the different levels of professional services available to the client or donor. The advisor must also be able to articulate this model to his or her service team, to referral sources, and to other providers and stakeholders.

Finally, the professional advisor must develop the capability of actually delivering a multi-tiered model of service to the clients or donors he or she serves. There's little point in talking the talk if he or she can't walk the walk.

# the transition from level one

In this section, we're going to spend some time going over the basic principles, tools, and vision of Level-Two client service. As we go, you'll see that the transition from Level One is natural, because Level-One skills are incorporated, not rejected, at Level Two. Of course, you will continue to provide financial, legal, and philanthropic products and services. Of course, you must continue to be the master of the numbers, the rules and regulations, the sharp analytics of Level One. None of that changes or goes away. The difference is that these products and services will take shape within a more complete context, humanly speaking.

Instead of being prepackaged goods that must be sold to the client or donor in the formulaic manner typical of Level-One transactions, they'll become the answers to essential questions of meaning that the client or donor may not even have articulated yet. It is a key function of the Level-Two advisor to help clients and donors to identify, articulate, and resolve these questions in philanthropic, financial, and estate plans that take into account much more than the client's or donor's material wealth.

# the life circle

Financial and estate planners and philanthropic professionals traditionally have focused on money and property as the defining elements of a client's or donor's wealth. But consider this: If your house was on fire, and you had time to save only one possession, which do you think it would be: the cash in the top drawer of the dresser or your family albums with the only photos of your children as babies?

Money has value, but only quantitative value. It is the sole currency of Flatland, but we who live in the human world know that many things hold far greater value than money, and we readily would part company with all our money rather than lose something that holds tremendous emotional value for us. As the MasterCard commercials rightly recognize, we can buy many things of value with money, but some things are "priceless."

Now, here's a fascinating question for you as a professional: If you asked your clients or donors the "burning house" question, what would you expect their answers to be? Wouldn't you be surprised if even one of your clients said that he or she would forfeit the irreplaceable photo albums in order to save the cash?

If so, this means that you already recognize that real wealth is not limited to money and property; it's just that, until now, the wealth of a client's or donor's life—the admittedly greater wealth that belongs not to money but to family, history, relationships, purpose—this wealth has been "none of your business." It's personal; and traditional financial, estate, and philanthropic planning are largely impersonal. And this is exactly what changes when we enter the world of Level-Two client and donor service. It becomes personal indeed, to the point that the client's or donor's *most meaningful wealth* informs the decisions that determine how the client's or donor's money and property are managed, planned for, and perhaps donated.

It is crucial to understand that these areas of wealth, which Level-One client service largely ignores or, at best, regards as incidental, move to center stage in Level-Two client service. The ancillary questions that you may or may not have asked a client or donor earlier will now become the crucial, defining ones—questions about the things they treasure, such as their heritage, personal history, and values.

# The Life Circle

Before we discuss how you can do this, let's look at a map of what a client's comprehensive wealth typically includes. We call this map The Life Circle. It's actually a tremendously useful tool to have on the desk when talking to a client or donor as it illuminates in a highly visual way, the Level-Two axiom that a client's wealth is far more than his or her material assets. At this point, it also provides us with a map to show us how far we've already traveled in our departure from Flatland.

You can readily see that Level-One client service deals only with the upper left quadrant, the "Financial" area, essentially ignoring the other three areas as well as the areas in the center. This means that Flatland thinking has led us to ignore more than 75% of our potential usefulness as legal, financial, and philanthropic professionals whose purpose is to advise the client or donor in the management of his or her wealth.

Of course, we didn't realize this. We may have thought of the categories contained in the center and the upper right and lower quadrants as the province of genealogists, therapists, clergy—but certainly not the hard and impersonal lines

> The simple truth is, whatever a donor or client values is part of his or her wealth. Their most meaningful wealth informs the decisions relating to their money and property.

of financial advising. We simply haven't had the vision, concepts, methods, and tools needed to acknowledge and work with them. The simple truth is, whatever a client or donor values is part of his or her wealth. As such, it may directly or indirectly affect decisions involving any area of wealth, including finances.

As professional advisors, we're trained to focus on the financial, legal, investment, charitable giving, and tax issues that affect our clients' wealth. This is all good, solid, Level-One thinking. But we shortchange our clients and donors if the services we provide fail to take into account and appreciate their wealth as extending far beyond money and property alone; because the most significant wealth we possess as human beings is not material. Material wealth, considered in isolation, is devoid of any real or enduring meaning. If our services deal only with the client's or donor's money and property, and ignore the clients or donors as human beings, then those services are similarly devoid of any real or enduring value.

The Life Circle reminds us that clients and donors come to us with a purpose that defines them and connects them to a past, to people and places, cultures and traditions out of which they emerged into their present life. Each client or donor is part of a family that has shaped his or her identity, beliefs, and values. All belong to a larger human community through friends, work, the organizations to which they belong, and the causes they hold dear.

Through the stories of their past and their vision of the future, they naturally seek to learn and grow humanly, to live whatever spiritual life speaks to them, to be responsible and skillful stewards of their life's riches, to shape their destiny, and to move into ever deeper fulfillment of their life's meaning and purpose. Properly addressed, understood, and applied, these non-material assets imbue the client's or donor's material wealth with meaning and purpose, and establish real and lasting value in the professional relationship.

# the legacy circle

When we move into the realm of estate planning and end-of-life planning, we have a second map to help us and our clients and donors appreciate that there is so much more to leave and so much more to plan for than material wealth. The Legacy Circle uses the same perspective on the wholeness of a person's wealth and potential legacy as does The Life Circle with respect to his or her lifetime wealth.

Reduced to the mere transfer of financial assets, the Level-One concept of "legacy" can feel cold, impersonal, or even repulsive to many people. But as we leave Flatland and travel to the three-dimensional world of Level Two, we find that "legacy" takes on a richer, more human meaning. There, it is not defined as building statues of ourselves or leaving buildings with our names on them, but as having an impact on the people and causes we care about most. Pericles was describing a Level-Two perspective when he said, *"What you leave behind is not what is engraved in stone monuments, but what is woven into the lives of others."*

## The Legacy Circle

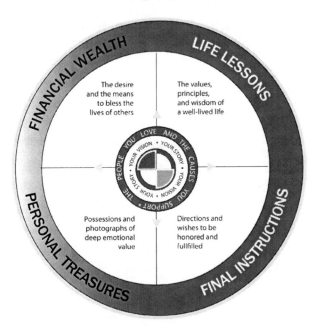

The Legacy Circle is consistent with the 2005 Allianz American Legacies Study, a research project that studied the perceptions of over 2,600 boomers and seniors. Comments by participants in the study reflect what most of our clients and donors already know about the legacy they wish to leave: that's it's about far more than how to reduce taxes and divvy up the money and property they will leave behind.

*"Legacy is what you leave behind when you're gone, and I don't think of it as money or possessions, more like what you teach of your values and your morals to your children."*

*"Legacy is memories and accomplishments and items that you pass on, and the emotional bonds that they hold for you."*

*"Legacy is the passing on of facts, stories, and unique works of your life to those who are important to you and there are tangible reminders to your family that may make them smile."*

*"Legacy is the rippling effect of possessions, money, children, beliefs, stories and deeds one leaves behind after death . . . continued through the generations."*

[
**How we live is inseparably connected to the legacy we leave.**
]

That study identified four "pillars" of a well-rounded legacy, which are reflected in the four main quadrants of The Legacy Circle. The Legacy Circle helps clients and donors to appreciate, and us to remember, that a well-designed legacy plan provides for several components woven into a unified tapestry.

Beyond its financial aspects, legacy can include a compilation of the client's or donor's life-lessons, such as their guiding values, principles, and wisdom—insight accumulated over decades. It can also include end-of-life and after-death wishes and instructions for loved ones, and the tender handling and sharing of personal treasures of deep emotional value. When the non-financial components of a legacy plan are integrated with and underwritten by the financial components of that plan, the impact of a client's or donor's legacy can be magnified and multiplied.

The Life Circle and The Legacy Circle are visual reminders that we humans are so much more than our bank accounts. They help us to remember what's most important, and to make sure that we acknowledge, appreciate, and honor this in the way we provide service.

# the life circle and the legacy circle together

"How," the thoughtful and observant student may inquire, "do The Life Circle and The Legacy Circle fit together or interact with each other?" What a delightful question indeed!

At an abstract level—thinking of them as graphic images—we can combine these two models by imagining a three-dimensional globe. Each of the quadrants becomes a fourth of a hemisphere, and the circles at the center of each circle become layers within the core of the sphere. That perspective, we shall shortly see, pushes us forward into a Level-Three world as outlined in the next chapter.

In the real world—applying the two models to actual human beings—the combination of the two circles helps us clearly recognize the profound truth that *how we live is inseparably connected to the legacy we leave.*

In his book *The Seven Habits of Highly Effective People,* Stephen R. Covey teaches the difficulty of "talking our way out of problems we have behaved ourselves into." This is similar to the old maxim that "I can't hear what you say because what you do rings so loudly in my ears." Thus, to live a purposeful, values-centered life, we must consider its long-term impact on others; and to truly change our legacy, we must change our life. We will consider this further in the next chapter's discussion of Level Three

# stories: the language of level two

The Life Circle and The Legacy Circle give us the map, but the map isn't the territory. How are we to traverse this rich, new terrain in which the client or donor is recognized as a human being rather than a column of numbers, and his or her wealth includes all the things the client or donor values? The answer is as simple as it is profound in practice: by listening to, learning from, and appreciating the client's *stories*.

Story is the key to a Level-Two practice. You actually begin to make the transition from Level One when you become willing to meet clients or donors on this common ground of sharing and listening to stories about what the client or donor has been through, what events shaped and influenced his or her values, and what matters most. You'll be shifting from trying to get the client or donor to understand why he needs your product or service, to understanding who the client or donor is. This new direction is so basic that there isn't an area of your practice that won't be deeply affected by it.

This is true for at least two reasons: First, **the stories of our experiences form the reality in which all of us live our lives.** And second, **story is our native language, our common mother tongue.**

# stories: the reality we live in

Who we each are as a person is defined not by what has happened to us, but by how we remember and describe what has happened to us, that is, by the stories we tell about what has happened to us. We have the inherent ability as human beings to choose our response to what the world does to us and to assign our own meanings to the world's actions and our responses. Consequently, we are not the events of our lives; rather, we are the sum total of the stories we hold on to and tell about the events of our lives.

Every event in life is subject to dozens if not hundreds of different interpretations. String together the millions of events that make up even one year in our lives, and we start to see that the possible combinations of interpretations are infinite. How then are we to make sense of the world around us?

I believe we do so by turning those millions of events into stories and then by living our lives according to the stories we have created around those events. In the words of the French author Jean-Paul Sartre: *"A man is always a teller of tales, he lives surrounded by his stories and the stories of others, he sees everything that happens to him through them, and he tries to live his own life as if he were telling a story."* Similarly, Canadian Dan Yashinsky wrote: *"The tales we cherish are tools for making sense of our journey."*

Over time, these stories become the reality we live in, much like the water fish swim in. Our lives become not the string of events that have happened to us, but the stories we tell about that string of events.

This is evidenced by listening to two people who have survived a common traumatic episode. One of them may say, "Oh, what a terrible experience! My life will never be the same. It has ruined everything." The other, having experienced the very same event, may say, "Yes, it was terrible, but just look at how blessed I am to have come out of it alive, and look at how much I learned in the process."

I observed this phenomenon firsthand when I went to Biloxi, Mississippi, in September of 2005, just three weeks after Hurricane Katrina decimated the area.

*I was one of several hundred men from our church who rode charter buses all night from Orlando to Biloxi to help clean up the devastation following Hurricane Katrina. Our group was sent to a poor area in East Biloxi about a mile from the ocean. In this area, the modest houses were still standing, but the water had flooded into them up to their attics. Everything inside that was not destroyed by the storm surge was ruined by the heat and humidity, because they had been barricaded off and closed up during the three weeks since the hurricane.*

*Because I have no particularly useful handy-man skills, I was assigned to one of the so-called "muck-out crews." Our job was to carry everything from the flooded houses and pile the whole moldy mess into giant mounds near the street where it could be hauled away. Then we would rip out the water-logged cabinets and the soggy sheet rock, exposing the studs with the hope that eventually they would dry out and the owners could rebuild.*

*It was heart-breaking to see people who had so little to start with, lose literally everything they owned in the world. Many we met in the neighborhood were understandably depressed, dejected, and angry because of their suffering and misfortune.*

*One of the families we helped was an older black couple. Their house was a bit larger than others in the area, but they too had lost everything. Although their experiences during the storm and in the aftermath were equally as harrowing and tragic as their neighbors, their attitudes were completely different.*

*As we worked to put all their ruined possessions on the street, the husband opened up and told me what had happened. He said they had built their house a year or so after Hurricane Camille devastated the Mississippi Gulf Coast in 1969. They had designed their house to stand at least a foot higher than the high water mark for Camille, and thus they assumed they would be safe at home when Katrina hit. Unfortunately, the water quickly rose past the high water mark for Camille and began to flood their house. When the water was waist deep in the house, they decided they'd better get out.*

*Neither one of the couple could swim, but their adult daughter who was with them was a strong swimmer. She went outside in the thick of the storm and, as luck would have it, found a small boat being blown down the street. She was able to retrieve it and bring it back to the porch. She helped her parents and their dog get into the boat. They then set off for a relative's two-story house a few blocks away. The winds and rain were fierce, and it was difficult for them to control the boat. They saw a woman they recognized clinging to a lamppost, but they were unable to get to her. They never saw her again.*

*With hard work and fervent prayer, they managed to make it to their relative's house. By the time they got there, the water was already above the windows of the first floor. Their daughter jumped out of the boat, broke out one of the first floor windows, swam up inside the house, and found the stairwell. She went to a second floor window, and pulled her parents in through that window. They rode out the storm in the second floor of the relative's house.*

*Leaving their house turned out to be a smart decision because the water ended up rising above the level of the ceiling. In a nearby house, a large family tried to stay in their house by wearing life jackets. Unfortunately, when the water rose past the level of the ceiling, they were pinned between the water and the ceiling and all were drowned.*

*Like everyone in the neighborhood, this courageous family lost everything they owned. Our crew of two dozen men spent more than a day hauling their possessions and piling them on the street and then stripping out the waterlogged sheet rock. But unlike their neighbors, who were bitter and miserable, they were thankful for our help and intensely grateful for what they saw as God's grace in helping them survive the storm. They said, "Yes we did lose everything, but we still have our lives. That's what matters most of all. God spared us and we can start again."*

> **To move to Level Two is to step beyond our world of calculations, analytics, products, and quick-fixes, and into their world of stories, relationships, values, and long-term solutions.**

This was a shared event with common experiences, but very different stories. Added together, these story-experiences constitute the themes of our lives, and of our clients' and donors' lives. Over time, who we are becomes inseparable from the stories we tell about who we are. *"'Who are you?' someone asks. 'I am the story of myself,' comes the answer."* (M. Scott Momaday) The acclaimed Nigerian novelist, Chinua Achebe, has written: *"We create stories and stories then create us. It is a rondo."* Clarissa Pinkola Estés expressed much the same sentiment when she said, *"The stories have grown the storytellers, grown them into who they are."*

Thus it is perfectly natural; if we want to understand our clients and donors in depth, if we want to see them and know them as more than a balance sheet or a set of possessions, then we come to know them through the narratives of their lives.

Because of our professional training, we advisors live primarily in a world of numbers; our clients and donors, as human beings, live primarily in a world of stories. Therefore, the essence of moving from Level-One transactions to Level-Two engagements is for us to step beyond our world of calculations, analytics, products, and quick-fixes, and meet them in their world of stories, relationships, values, and long-term solutions.

It is critical that we remember when we are operating at Level Two, our Level-One skills and tools will continue to be essential to delivering those long-term solutions. Becoming a Level-Two advisor is no excuse for professional sloppiness or lack of technical excellence. But that excellence is now provided within a richly human context of meaning, understanding and purpose, attained through the medium of the client's or donor's stories.

# stories: our common native language

The second reason why story is essential to understanding who the client or donor is and why every area of your practice will be deeply affected by it is because **story is our native language, our mother tongue**. This is true both on a global and a personal level.

As human beings, regardless of nationality, race, creed, gender, or age, we have for thousands of years used story to share important information with our tribe. While the shaman around the community campfire may have been replaced by the actors and announcers on the family television or, more recently by the characters in the videos on YouTube or the posts on Facebook, we as a species have turned to story to learn what we need to pay attention to in our world.

Looking at our personal lives, until we were a dozen or so years old, story is how we looked at and made sense of the world. It is how our parents taught us right from wrong. It is how they coaxed us to bed at night. It is how we played (cops and robbers, cowboys and Indians, Barbie and Ken) and how we learned. It is how we connected and communicated with those around us.

It wasn't until later that we learned how to be analytical. Even then, it wasn't until law school, business school, or professional training that much of our native expression in story was replaced. But a part of us—and a big part of our clients and donors—still longs for story, this most human of media.

I've learned first-hand this power of communicating in our common native language. I have a college degree in Portuguese, which I earned after I had spent a number of years in Brazil speaking Portuguese most of the time. I subsequently lived for 20 years in places where no other person spoke Portuguese; consequently, I lost the ability to speak comfortably in this second language.

Now I live in the Orlando area and have frequent opportunities to speak Portuguese. But because of that 20-year hiatus, I have to work hard to be fully present in the conversation. I notice how tense I become as I struggle to remember how to express a certain thought, or conjugate a particular verb, or construct agreement between nouns and adjectives. I'm sure that I often miss the meanings of the other person's statements, and certainly the nuances of tone and expression.

Occasionally the person I'm speaking with, recognizing that his or her English is better than my Portuguese, switches the conversation to English. It's amazing for me to notice how I immediately relax, begin to enjoy the exchange of ideas, and grasp the whole conversation.

Clients and donors may encounter that stress when meeting with a financial advisor, estate planner, or philanthropic professional, especially as we discuss money, taxes, investments, planned-giving tactics, death, or disability. As if this weren't daunting enough, we often speak to them in our legal-ese, financial planner-ese, planned giving-ese, or analytical-ese. If we're perceptive, we may notice how tense they become as they struggle to understand us, and to express themselves in the language of our Flatland world.

We've all had the experience of being in a situation where all those around us were speaking in a language we didn't understand. We may have felt uneasy and perhaps ignorant, but certainly inhibited in our ability to contribute. We expect to have such feelings where we're traveling on the other side of the globe, but not when we visit the office of an estate planner, financial advisor, or philanthropic professional in our own community.

I have learned that if we as professional advisors switch from the traditional Level-One idiom into the clients' or donors' native language of story, the whole tone of the conversation changes. They relax, they enjoy the exchange of ideas, and they grasp more of what we're seeking to share with them. More importantly, they begin to share who they really are with us.

You may find that the best way to get comfortable with stories is to begin telling your own to someone you trust. Many of the tools described in this section for use with clients and donors are tools that you can apply to your life as well. In a Level-Two practice, the line between personal and professional is not nearly as hard as it has been traditionally among financial professionals. In fact, it's safe to say that your success as a Level-Two advisor will depend on your ability to share *your* narrative asset wealth with your clients or donors—your experiences and stories, your wisdom and discernment, your compassion and creativity.

Naturally, there are many things that you and your client will not elect to share with each other for many reasons. It is, however, essential that you become comfortable with the language of story, and be willing to show up humanly in the truth of your stories. We teach best by example, and by doing this, you demonstrate in the most powerful way possible your qualifications and trustworthiness as a Level-Two advisor.

# stories: the power of human connection

It's hard to overstate the power that story has to create an immediate and lasting connection between any two human beings. One of the things I learned from a project of capturing clients' life stories on tape and preserving them with the photographs and documents from their personal histories, is how deeply and quickly one person will bond with another, even a total stranger, who demonstrates a genuine interest in that person's life and experiences.

We show how much we value another person simply by asking what we at SunBridge call "story-leading questions," then listening generously, with

[
### When clients and advisors share the language of story, they become more fully human in each other's eyes.
]

undivided attention. In this simplest and most natural of human exchanges, we can create amazing and lasting trust and friendship in a matter of a few minutes.

Client and donor stories drawn from their most meaningful experiences are a gold mine of understanding for the attentive and caring advisor. The client's or donor's values and priorities are laid out for the discerning to see and appreciate, far more effectively than can be achieved through the most cleverly designed questionnaire. Story provides a context within which the client's concerns and problems can be identified, pointing the way, often immediately, to deeply human and gratifying solutions.

When the client and advisor share the language of story, they become more fully human in each other's eyes. The client or donor who is invited to share his or her life experiences as part of the advisor's search for answers to their problems feels valued, heard, and understood. And the advisor's counsel acquires a correspondingly greater value, in every sense.

# meaning of money stories

Since the prospective client or donor has usually agreed to see the advisor about some issue related to finances, I've found it helpful, after learning something of who the client or donor is, where he came from, and how he ended up here, to invite him to share with me what I call "meaning of money" stories. These are experiences that have helped the client or donor define what money means to him, which in turn dictates what types of planning he is open to considering.

The reason these particular stories matter is because each one of us has a different relationship with money. We each have a unique definition of what money means and that definition, that relationship, was created over our lifetime through a long series of personal experiences with money.

In order to understand what money means to a person, the best way is to have them recall and share the experiences by which the definition of the "meaning of money" was formed for them. This is a far more effective and enjoyable way to understand what money means for a client or donor than to use some sort of a questionnaire. Even the most cleverly designed questionnaire is not nearly as effective in helping us understand the nuances and emotions associated with money for our clients and donors as hearing in their own words the experiences they have had and the stories they have fashioned about those experiences.

If we as advisors understand these stories and are able to connect the dots with clients and donors, we can be much more effective in helping them address their money issues. This is true whether we work in the field of financial planning, retirement planning, estate planning, philanthropic planning, investing, or any other related area.

The meaning of money, because it is so unique and individual, is very often heard between the lines of the stories our clients and donors tell. Much of what we understand about money is not on the conscious level. It resides somewhere deep inside of us and therefore, sharing stories that are rich with meaning and understanding, is in fact the most effective way to get at that definition.

Often those stories are about something that happened early in the client's or donor's life when he discovered—often dramatically—what money meant in the family or community in which he grew up. Sometimes the story takes place early in the client's or donor's married life, when he abruptly learned that money meant something entirely different to his spouse.

It is very important, I have found, to make sure that this process is done naturally and comfortably. That can sometimes best be done when we share one of those experiences from our own lives first. To get this ball rolling, I often share one of my experiences, when a new pair of shoes helped me understand the meaning of money in the Farnsworth family.

*I grew up on a small dairy farm in northwest New Mexico, one of twelve children (plus another brother who had died before we all came together as a blended family.) We had a small farm bordering the San Juan River across from the Navajo Reservation. Things were difficult for us financially with so many mouths to feed, but we raised most of our own food. We had dairy cows, chickens, pigs, a beef cow, gardens, and orchards, so we were able to provide for ourselves that way. Shoes and clothes, however, posed a real challenge for my parents. Fourteen pairs of feet were a lot to keep in shoes!*

*One of the many blessings we had was our Uncle Jack, who had a trading post on the Navajo Reservation, where we could buy clothes and shoes wholesale. Every month or so our family went out to the trading post and got the things we needed. A trading post is not exactly Saks Fifth Avenue; it's a store stocked with only the basic things of rural life, a general store with sheep and goats, and rugs, jewelry, and the like.*

*Before we went to the trading post we invariably had a family meeting to decide who would get what. My father was not one to brook any sort of "confusion," as he called it, when we got to the store.*

*I remember when I was eleven, I'd decided that I was due a new pair of shoes, but the family council had decided that I was not going to get a new pair of shoes, and this left me anything but pleased. I can still remember sitting in the back seat of the car in the driveway, the whole family ready to go, and we couldn't leave because I was throwing a fit. My father stood in the driveway reasoning with me through the open window of the car.*

*Finally, after some minutes of unsuccessfully trying to persuade me to be happy about what I was going to get, he did something unexpected. He lifted up his shoe and laid it on the window seal of the car, then turned it over to show me the bottom. These were his good Sunday shoes and the bottom was totally broken out. There wasn't enough leather there to re-sole them, even if we had had the money, and he, the inclination. He looked me straight in the eye and he said, "Scott, we can't afford to buy me new shoes today, and we can't afford to buy you new shoes, either. Do you understand, son?"*

*Did I ever! In an instant, through the image powerfully conveyed by*
*that single, unforgettable, moment, I understood what money meant in our*
*family. That moment was indelible. It still shapes the way I think of money;*
*it still affects the way I respond when my children ask me for things.*

Each one of us has had experiences that define what money means to us.
As Level-Two advisors, we take the time to understand what money means to
our clients by listening to their stories.

# managing expectations at level two

One of the reasons why sharing meaning of money stories is an effective
way to open a larger, story-based relationship with a client or donor is because
it fits naturally within the set of expectations clients or donors bring with them.
That is, even if they are in a Level-One mindset because of past conditioning,
they come to us expecting to talk about money. Thus, when we start asking about
their meaning of money stories, it doesn't feel to them like we are changing the
subject or steering the conversation in an odd direction.

This is an example of meeting our clients and donors where they are and
then inviting them to a higher place. It's all about managing expectations. In
SunBridge, we use a story about an experiment with two groups of chimpanzees
to teach this concept.

If I were to ask you to guess what a chimpanzee's favorite food is, you would
probably guess it is bananas. If you did, you would be correct. If I were to ask you
to guess what a chimpanzee's second favorite food is, you probably wouldn't have
a clue. You would probably guess some other kind of fruit, or nuts, or perhaps
something sweet. The correct answer is lettuce. Believe it or not, chimpanzees like
lettuce almost as much as bananas. Given a choice, a chimpanzee will pick lettuce
nearly as often as bananas.

A group of zoologists, aware that chimpanzees like bananas and lettuce
almost equally, conducted an interesting experiment using two similar groups of
chimps. They placed one group in a closed room with a door leading out to a cage.

In the cage they placed a wooden box under which they placed several heads of lettuce. They then opened the door to the room and allowed the chimpanzees into the cage. The chimpanzees discovered the box, lifted it up, and found the lettuce, their second favorite food. As you might imagine, they were delighted and began to eat the lettuce contentedly.

The second group of chimpanzees was placed in a similar environment, with one exception. Between the room and the cage, there was a window with open curtains through which the chimps could see into the cage. The zoologists, in plain sight of the chimpanzees, placed a bunch of bananas under the wooden box. Then they closed the curtains, removed the bananas, and replaced them with heads of lettuce. They opened the door to the room and the chimpanzees were allowed into the cage. They went straight for the box, lifted it up, and discovered lettuce, their second favorite food. How do you suppose they responded?

Rather than being happy to find their second favorite food, these chimpanzees, unlike the first group, went absolutely berserk. They shrieked in anger, shredded the lettuce, and stamped on it. They went totally "bananas!"

Remember, these chimpanzees hadn't discovered under the box something they hated; they had found lettuce, their second favorite food. But instead of eating it contentedly like the first group, they went ballistic. What was the difference?

Obviously, the difference was their expectations. The first group had no expectation of finding bananas under the box, and thus they were quite happy when they discovered lettuce there. The second group, however, expected to find bananas. When they found lettuce instead, their expectations were thwarted.

To the degree that we can extrapolate from chimp behavior to human behavior, there is a significant lesson here. When people's expectations aren't met, even when they are offered something they would otherwise cherish, they will often become irrational and even angry.

My own experience has taught me that one of the keys to beginning a successful Level-Two relationship is to manage expectations. If their focus is on money issues, I need to honor that focus by meeting them there. But if I hope to move our relationship to Level Two, I must move into the realm of stories—their meaningful stories. Since they expect to talk about money and I want to share stories, it's quite natural for me to ask about their meaning of money stories.

It also helps in pivoting from Level-One expectations to Level-Two relationships if I can identify for the client or donor what I have learned from his or her meaning of money stories and demonstrate how that insight will create better outcomes for the him or her. When it's obvious that sharing stories will lead to the results they are seeking, it's easy to move on to other stories besides those strictly about money.

# other important stories

Our clients and donors also have stories about their family, giving, sharing, community, heritage, and many other important facets of their life. Indeed, every person has many stories, however unwitting, unformulated, or even forsaken they may be. Hidden within each story is a compass heading for deeply fulfilling financial choices and directions. Let's take a look at how this compares to Level-One advising:

---

### Level Two: Meaning
Relationships, Understanding, Context, Perspective & Dialogue,
Long-Term Solutions

### STORY

### Level One: Money
Transactions, Documents & Products, Formulas, Time & Advice,
Short-Term Answers

---

Let me share another story that isn't directly about money to show you how deeply our values are shaped by our memories of formative experiences, and how story provides a bridge for crossing from a Level-One to a Level-Two relationship:

*My mother died of cancer when she was 32 years old, and I was eight, the oldest of her six surviving children. When I turned 12, my father took me aside and said, "I have something for you from your mother." Then he handed me a two-page letter that she had written to me not long before she passed, leaving instructions for my father that it be given to me on my twelfth birthday, an age marking a rite of passage into manhood in our family's faith.*

*My mother's words of love, tenderness, and wise counsel, penned in that brief letter, touched me to the core, and continue to do so now, decades later. She talked to me about making good choices in my teenage years, and the importance of staying close to family and friends. She told me how much she cherished our faith, and she expressed a deep hope that I would continue to value it too. Most of all, she wanted me to know that, whatever choices I might make in my life, she would always love me.*

*I did not inherit money or property from my mother. What little my parents had materially was spent on my mother's long and arduous medical treatment. To this day, however, I value that letter immeasurably more than anything financial she could have left me. It is living proof that, even in her hour of suffering, knowing that she would not live to see me grow up, she thought of me, loved me, and found a way to make sure I knew it.*

*I remember too vividly how frail and thin she was at the end, her body emaciated by the cancer, as though it were physically drawing her from this world. Sometimes I imagine how hard she struggled to finish the six letters she knew she had to write before her strength abandoned her entirely. Now that I am the parent of six children, I think about her emotions as she fought to pen the last paragraphs, or perhaps the last words of my letter. And I'm beginning to understand just how much her example of courage, love, heroic devotion, and selflessness mean to me and those around me.*

[
**We can't really be valuable to our clients until we value them, and we can't value them if we don't know who they are; that is, if we don't know their stories.**
]

Now, if I were a client of yours, what would hearing such a story tell you about what I value? And how useful would this knowledge be to you in making uniquely useful and fulfilling recommendations to me? You see, we can't really be valuable to our clients until we value them, and we can't value them if we don't know who they are; that is, if we don't know their stories.

As an estate planning attorney, I've drafted thousands of wills and trusts. I realize how important it is to provide for the ultimate distribution of one's material assets and the settling of one's financial and legal affairs. Beyond this, however, I know that if all we do is provide for our financial legacy, we will have left most of the job undone. Material wealth is only the first part of what we have to pass on to others.

Our life legacy is far more; it is the living declaration of who we are as unique human beings, a chronicle of the path we've traveled, and a bridge of values, vision, wisdom, and experience that can enrich those we love and many others into the future, perhaps with an influence that never dies.

Here's another example of the power of story to reveal the client as human being. In this one, we'll take it a step further so you can see how the client's story gets translated into Level-Two client service:

*Mr. Jacobs came to see our firm when he was 88 years old. With an estate worth approximately $9 million, he was looking down the barrel of an estate tax of about $5 million, largely because of some botched planning that had been previously done for him.*

*After reviewing the situation, I asked Mr. Jacobs if he were open to the idea of charitable giving. He was. "I've been a lifelong member of Rotary, and I'd be happy to donate $2,000. My deceased wife was an active member of a sewing club. I could give them $3,000 in her memory."*

*I decided to save the discussion of charitable giving for another time. Instead, I started getting to know Mr. Jacobs. He was a good man with a remarkable story. It seems he had grown up and spent his long life on two pieces of ground. Born in upstate New York, he had lived on a farm there until he was ten. Then his family moved to Central Florida, and bought a small farm near the town of Ocoee, where he had lived ever since.*

*He'd certainly had his share of misfortune. As a boy in New York, he had lost an eye in a farming accident. He also had contracted polio, so one of his legs was withered, and he walked with a pronounced limp. He had been married for many years, but his wife had passed away about five years before I met him. He had one child, a daughter in her mid-50s who had not fulfilled any particular ambitions, and still waited tables at a local restaurant. She had two children, a son and a daughter, both in their early 20s at the time, and both involved heavily with illicit drug use. The son had been arrested for dealing drugs for his father, Mr. Jacob's ex-son-in-law, who was serving time in a Federal prison. Mr. Jacob's granddaughter also was pregnant; Mr. Jacobs did not know who the father might be.*

*In view of all this, and understandably, while Mr. Jacobs wanted to make sure that his child's and his grandchildren's needs were met, he certainly had no intention of leaving them $9 million. Mr. Jacobs had worked hard all his life. When he was a teenager, he and his father had built a service station on their property, which Mr. Jacobs had operated since he was 18. He told me interesting stories about sleeping in the station all night, so in case a car drove by at two in the morning, he would be there to sell them a quarter's worth of gas. At one point, he owned his own tanker truck, worked in the station all day, then drove the tanker to Tampa at night (which, in those days took four or five hours), filled up, drove back, unloaded the tanker truck in time to open the station early in the morning, and then worked all day again taking care of customers.*

*Ocoee, where Mr. Jacobs lived, might fairly be described as a stepchild of Orange County. It's a town with a hard-luck story, much like Mr. Jacobs's. In the early 20s, there had been a race riot there on Election Day. Several people were killed—an incident that had stigmatized the town and still cast a shadow over it many years later. Early in the Great Depression, the town lost its bank, leaving it with no source of lending for businesses looking to put down roots and grow there.*

*Mr. Jacobs told me that he knew a number of merchants who went to the bank of a nearby town seeking a loan, and were refused because the bank did not want to support businesses that would compete with those in its own town. Mr. Jacobs chose to use this setback as an opportunity. In the 60s, he and a few Rotary Club buddies opened a bank in Ocoee. He donated the property on which the bank was built. One merger followed another, until eventually Mr. Jacobs's investment of land for the bank had returned the current value of his estate—$9 million.*

*Mr. Jacobs and I spent a good bit of time together. I helped him capture and articulate some of these stories. I wanted to make sure that, in addition to protecting the financial resources he had, we also preserved the rest of his wealth—who he was, what he had learned, and the values that had guided him to his hard-won wisdom. And I wanted to ensure that this wisdom would somehow be passed along intact to those who would follow him, even though, at the time, they did not seem particularly interested in what he had to say.*

*As we talked one afternoon, I was struck by an insight into what might be important for Mr. Jacobs. He was describing his friendships and associations with citizens of Ocoee, his adopted hometown, and it suddenly seemed clear to me that this was the key. "Mr. Jacobs," I asked, "what would you think if we could take the money that otherwise would go to the IRS, and instead direct it into an account that you and those you trust could dispense for projects in Ocoee?"*

*He looked at me, and asked, "What do you mean?" "We could take the money that otherwise would have to be paid in taxes, and see to it that it was spent to improve the town and the lives of the people there." He was intrigued. "Give me an example," he said, leaning forward. "Well," I said, "suppose that the elementary school needed new playground equipment. We could take some of the money that we had set aside in a special fund—one that you and those you trust could control—and buy the equipment. If the girls needed a new softball field to play on, you could finance its construction. If you just wanted to make the Christmas parade extra special one year, you could direct funds to do just that."*

[
**His gift made a significant difference in the little town he loved so much, but more importantly, it infused great energy and purpose into his life.**
]

*Mr. Jacobs's eyes grew wide; I could see he was imagining the possibilities. "We could do that?" he asked. "Indeed, we could. And it wouldn't take away anything from your family, because the money we'd be using to set up the fund would otherwise just have gone to the government." Mr. Jacobs sat back in his chair with a deeply gratified grin. "This is exciting" he said, and a new mood of enthusiasm came over him. He was already planning what he would do with the money we would use to establish this fund for the town he so loved.*

*Rather than giving $2,000 to the Rotary Club or $3,000 to his wife's sewing circle, Mr. Jacobs ended up contributing $5 million. The money was used, as we had discussed, to create a fund to benefit the city of Ocoee—a fund that would be controlled by him and those he trusted, and be used expressly to support worthwhile community projects for that town, in keeping with the things that Mr. Jacobs felt were most important.*

*With his wife gone, and appropriate arrangements made to care for his child and grandchildren, his remaining great love was the town of Ocoee. The difference that this Level-Two advising made for him and for the citizens of Ocoee may well extend beyond the foreseeable future, benefiting countless generations to come.*

During his remaining years, although he still walked with a limp, Mr. Jacobs had a new spring in his step. His gift made a significant difference in the little town he loved so much, but more importantly, it infused great energy and purpose into his life. He found what made him come alive and then he went and did something about it. He truly found himself.

This in turn energized those around him. His family, his friends, his team of advisors—all were touched and changed by his generosity and his new focus. His gift was a gift that kept on giving.

# level-two client service

In the last chapter, we identified the cornerstones of a Level-One Practice. To review, they are:

**Method:** Mind
**Main Focus:** Money
**View of Client/Donor:** Balance Sheet
**Vision:** Quick-Fixes

Now, the cornerstones of Level-Two client service are very different:

**Method:** Heart
**Main Focus:** Meaning
**View of Client/Donor:** Whole Person
**Vision:** Connection

Let's take a brief look at each of these as a key element of Level-Two client service.

## Heart

*"It is only with the heart that one can see rightly; what is essential is invisible to the eye."*
*—Antoine de Saint-Exupéry*

Level-Two client service is both an intuitive and analytical method, an art as well as a science. The Level-Two advisor is mindful of the client's values and feelings at every point, and uses these as a compass heading to stay on course. In order to meet the client at this level, the advisor must be willing to listen with his heart to the client's story.

## Meaning

*"For the meaning of life differs from man to man, from day to day and from hour to hour. What matters, therefore, is not the meaning of life in general but rather the specific meaning of a person's life at a given moment." —Viktor Frankl*

Meaning is a mysterious thing. We can endure almost anything if we can find meaning in it. Meaning informs and shapes our life, our choices, our reactions and responses, our very identity. When we work directly with whatever is meaningful to a client, we begin to see the world—including our work—through the client's eyes. With this insight, our role as someone who can deliver a deeper fulfillment of meaning and purpose is apparent. To become useful at this level is really to become indispensable—not only to a client, but also to a child, spouse, or friend. This is why meaning is the main focus of the Level-Two relationship.

## Whole Person

*"I sense [in some] a desire to pass on something more than the material wealth they have accumulated. They want to pass on something of the spirit of who they are. They seem to have come to an understanding that net worth means more than just a static, bottom line number. —Dr. Barrie Sanford Greiff*

Because Level-Two service centers on values and meaning, it aims to cultivate the client as a whole person. Financial directions are not just decreed in a vacuum of numbers and regulations, but made to conform to those things the client holds dear.

## Connection

*"They may forget what you said, but they will never forget how you made them feel."*
—Carl W. Buechner

The vision that informs Level-Two client service is *connection*—with the client, his story, his future, the things that matter to him most. When this connection is made between client and advisor, the advisor becomes what might be considered a professional friend. Working together, they serve the larger purpose of the meaning of the client's life story; together they serve, support, and encourage its fullest expression.

These are the defining features of Level-Two client service. As soon as they're introduced into the client/advisor conversation, the relationship begins to shift from a hit-and-run, quick-fix interaction to one that has the potential of becoming a lifelong partnership.

# ten truths

At Level Two, we're building a lifelong relationship with the client or donor based on the significance of the client's or donor's stories for his or her life, and helping to chart a vision for the future based on that significance. As a context and framework for the cultivation of this vision, SunBridge articulates ten fundamental truths, which we suggest you keep in mind. These truths will help you identify the direction to take in advising your client. The left side of the table lists the sorts of interests and concerns clients and donors invariably bring once the door opens to a Level-Two relationship. The right side gives you the corresponding pragmatic response to these interests and concerns. As simple as these truths may seem, they can serve as powerful compass headings to keep you on course:

## Ten Truths

| | |
|---|---|
| I have concerns about money and property . . . | So help me find financial security and peace of mind. |
| I know I'm much more than my money and property . . . | So help me use all my resources to create greater abundance and purpose in my life. |
| I love my family . . . | So show me how to build stronger bridges to the people I love. |
| I like to feel important . . . | So pay attention to me and listen well. |
| I like to feel smart . . . | So talk to me in plain English and be clear. |

| | |
|---|---|
| I don't like feeling manipulated . . . | So help me understand my real needs and stop trying to sell me something I don't need. |
| I have a lifetime of stories . . . | So help me share my experiences with you, so you'll understand who I am. |
| I have many hopes and dreams for the future . . . | So help me see clearly what the vision of my life can be. |
| I want to make a difference in the world . . . . | So help me act on the things that I find most significant. |
| I want to be remembered when I'm gone . . . | So help me pass on my values and preserve the meaning and stories of my life. |

# getting from here to there

So how can a financial advisor, an estate planner, or a philanthropic professional move confidently from the Flatland world of Level One to the multidimensional world of Level Two? Even though this shift employs story, the natural medium we all live in and our common native language, it's not always easy for us to make this change.

In many cases, vaulting permanently into the rewarding world of Level-Two advising demands work, commitment, and persistence. Getting to Level Two often requires us to hack our way through the underbrush of years and perhaps decades of Level-One indoctrination and training. It sometimes requires us to replace dozens of deeply imbedded old habits by gently cultivating new habits and then strengthening them over time.

Such a transformation is not an instantaneous event but is an ongoing process. It requires four essential ingredients that must be persistently applied and re-applied in generous quantities. They are: **1)** a new mind-set; **2)** a new skill-set; **3)** a new tool-set; and **4)** a new support-set. These four steps are illustrated in a teaching tool we use at SunBridge called "Taking Charge."

## Taking Charge

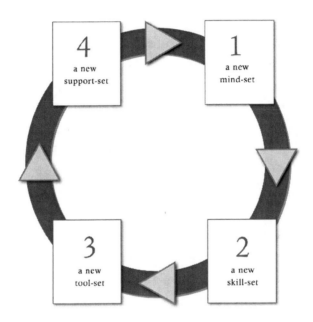

# a new mind-set

To successfully effect the transformation from Level One to Level Two, we must first develop *a new mind-set*. We must think differently about who we are, about who our clients or donors are, about what wealth is, about the purpose and meaning of our work, and about the value we are trying to create in the world. Until this mental shift happens, the conversion cannot really start to develop. Until we can truly see ourselves as operating comfortably and authentically in this new multi-dimensional realm, our transformation will not make much progress.

Without a soul-deep shift in our thinking, everything else we may attempt toward moving to Level Two will turn out to be shallow and artificial. Being a

[
**Being a Level-Two advisor is not a garb we put on for certain occasions, nor is it a set of techniques we employ for effect. It is a way of thinking, feeling, being.**
]

Level-Two advisor is not a garb we put on for certain occasions, nor is it a set of techniques we employ for effect. It is a way of thinking, a way of feeling, indeed, a way of being. It all begins with a new mind-set.

This whole book to this point has been designed to help us get our heads around the idea that both professional advisors and their clients and donors are ill-served when the traditional Flatland, Level-One model of planning is the only option available.

Instead, there is an alternative story-based approach that is more suitable for many clients and donors (and their advisors) because it addresses their deeper human concerns, it acknowledges that their real wealth is not limited to those things that can be tallied on a balance sheet, and it recognizes that many of the most important questions in planning cannot be answered with a number. In short, Level-Two planning produces better bottom-line results as well as better human results.

Another aspect of a new mind-set is the confidence that you can pull this off with your own clients or donors. Having read this far, you may be saying to yourself, "I hope what you say is true. I'd like to believe it could be true. It sounds right and feels right, and I'd love to work that way with many of my clients or donors. But I wonder if I can do it. I'm not sure I can offer this 'Level Two' approach in my own practice."

Such feelings are perfectly normal, especially before you've become familiar with the skills, tools, and support that we've developed at SunBridge to help advisors like you move confidently into the world of Level-Two advising. Rest assured, if you enjoy telling a story and can listen attentively to another telling his or her story, you have the core competency required to become a successful Level-Two Advisor.

# a new mind-set: two experts in the room

Another of the key mental shifts required to work successfully at Level Two is the understanding that we must work collaboratively with our clients, helping them to share the stories that are the raw materials for our work together and then to think with us about how to solve their problems and address their concerns.

As demonstrated in the earlier story about Mr. Jacobs, Level Two client service is rooted in a rich and meaningful dialogue between two human beings, two equals—not an aloof expert and a passive client or donor. Level-Two planning is inherently collaborative in nature. It is not something we lawyers or financial planners or planned giving professionals do *to* the client or donor, nor is it something we do *for* them; it is something we do *with* them.

Level-Two client or donor service requires that we understand when an advisor and a client or donor sit down together to plan, there are two experts in the room, not just one. We may be the expert on investments, insurance, taxes, legal documents, philanthropic giving strategies, public benefits, and the like, but clients and donors are the experts on their lives, their stories, their families, and their values.

All of our technical knowledge, which is absolutely critical to the success of the plan, is sadly worthless unless the client's or donor's knowledge and understanding of their life, story, family and values are effectively brought into the process and incorporated into every facet of the plan. Both perspectives and both sets of knowledge must be brought together in a seamless whole or the planning will ultimately fail.

This truth makes it crystal clear that we as advisors must bring another form of expertise to the table: the ability to create an environment in which the client or donor can freely share his or her stories, and can also think, speak, and contribute to the design of the plan as an equal partner with the advisor. We must be capable of drawing from them their very best thinking on the subject.

My dear friend Nancy Kline calls such an environment a Thinking Environment®. She teaches that without a Thinking Environment, the advisor will never be able to create the best possible plan because huge chunks of the solution will remain locked up inside the client or donor and his or her untold stories. In her book *More Time to Think,* she identifies ten ways of being with clients or donors that help create a Thinking Environment.

The most important of these is the quality of attention we give our clients or donors, listening without interruption but with boundless curiosity about where their thinking is going and where it will go next. It's also important to develop a sense of ease and an atmosphere of appreciation and equality. We must provide them appropriate information and sometimes give them courage to think beyond themselves and ask themselves challenging, incisive questions. On occasion we must reassure them that we are comfortable when their emotions surface. We must offer them a physical space that says, "You matter."

When we successfully do this, the result is the joint creation of something far beyond what either of us could have built on our own. The result is a plan that is both technically brilliant and humanly magnificent. The outcome is a rich and lasting relationship and a powerful and enduring solution. The outcome is an extension of their story in a beautiful new direction.

# a new skill-set

Once our thinking has shifted, the next step in the transformation process is to develop *a new skill-set.* Operating successfully at Level Two requires that we employ additional capabilities beyond those we used in Flatland. Level-One skills are not jettisoned as we are converted into a Level-Two advisor; we still need them just as much. But we must add additional strengths and talents to our repertoire.

Developing these new Level-Two skills is an on-going process that can last a lifetime, but fortunately we don't have to be perfect at all of them to get started. What we do need from the start is an attitude of openness and teach-ability, and a willingness to learn, experiment, and practice. It also helps to have patience with ourselves while in the learning curve, and the courage to dare to be ugly as our new skill-set is maturing.

> We must bring to the table the ability to create an environment in which the client or donor can freely think, speak, share, and contribute to the design of the plan as an equal partner.

Foremost among these key skills is the ability to work comfortably in the world of story; to engage artfully in the give and take of story sharing in a professional setting. There are at least three significant components to this skill-set: 1) the ability to coax meaningful stories from our clients and donors: 2) the ability to listen attentively and with discernment to their stories; and 3) the ability to craft and tell a wide variety of story-types. All of these components are interrelated and each plays off the others, but I'll address them one at a time.

# encouraging clients and donors to tell stories

While nearly all people are natural-born story tellers, most clients and donors likely have been conditioned to believe that sharing stories is inappropriate for the lawyer's office or in other professional settings, where numbers and analytics are king. As a result, we must cultivate the skill to let them know that when they are with us, it is OK to return to their native language of story. This happens most naturally when we use an abundance of stories to communicate with them and when we ask our clients and donors "story-leading questions."

Professional advisors who instruct, explain, demonstrate, persuade, and give examples using a wide variety of stories not only communicate more effectively than those who do not, they also make it more likely that their clients and donors will share their stories with the advisors. The advisor's stories speak to the story centers in the intuitive side of the clients' and donors' brains. There, they activate narrative thinking and encourage narrative speaking. Storytelling begets storytelling. Thus, the advisor's stories set the stage for client and donor stories.

Stories come in a wide variety of sizes, shapes, and colors, and serve a wide variety of purposes. (More about that in the 'using many different types of stories' section.) By becoming familiar and comfortable with a wide array of story types, a professional advisor can include several of them in his or her client meetings, thus making it easier for clients or donors to share their stories.

It also helps to ask lots of "story-leading questions." Some who hear the term mistakenly believe that such a question must call for a long, drawn-out answer including a protagonist, a plot, and a turning point leading to a resolution, a la the classic Aristotelian form of a story. Not so. A story-leading question is an open-ended question that can best be answered with a narrative, however brief. It is a question that invites one to respond by relating an event or set of events that are causally related.

We use such questions all the time in casual or social conversations, usually without being aware of it. For example, "How are you coping with this weather we've been having lately?" Or, "What are your plans for Labor Day weekend?" Or, "How was your drive to our office? Have any trouble in traffic?" But for some reason, we tend to forget how to use them when we get down to the "real business" of the client or donor meeting.

The key is to start weaving story-leading questions into all aspects of your client or donor meetings, even the analytical parts. After, "Let's run through the numbers on your balance sheet," you ask, "Tell me how you acquired that property?" or "What do you envision happening with that holding?" After, "Here's the schedule of specific charitable distributions to be included in your will," you say, "I'm interested in how you selected these recipients and these amounts," or "What do you hope will result from these gifts?" Obviously, once we've asked a story-leading question, it's extremely important that we then listen generously to their answers.

# the art of listening: the expert as listener

---

*"When people talk, listen completely. I have learned a great deal from listening carefully. Most people never listen." —Earnest Hemmingway*

---

Most people think that an expert is a person who knows a lot and gets paid to deliver brilliant answers. The essence of what he does is talk, right? Wrong. The so-called expert who can't or won't listen well — regardless of how smart he is — is more often than not useless:

- He gives the wrong answer because he misses important information.
- He gives the right answer to the wrong question.
- He gives the right answer but his answer is incomprehensible to the client or donor.
- He answers the obvious question but completely misses the real question.
- He gives the right answer but completely misses the human implications of both the question and the answer.
- He gives the right answer but his advice isn't followed because clients and donors don't trust him.

A real expert is an expert listener.

A real expert realizes that the quality of his answer is only as good as the quality of the information he hears. A real expert knows that if he doesn't hear the correct question or the real question, his answer — even though correct — will be largely worthless. A real expert recognizes that until clients or donors feel listened to and understood, his answers will be suspect and his recommendations will likely not be implemented.

A real expert understands that when he sits down with a client or donor, there are two experts in the room, not one. A real expert knows that to find the best answers in today's complex world, he must bring everyone's best thinking to bear on the issue at hand, not just his own. A real expert has the temperament and the tools to do so.

A real expert recognizes that, regardless of what others may call his line of work, he is really in the transformation business. Pine and Gilmore have demonstrated in their masterful book, *The Experience Economy*, that the highest-value product a business can deliver is not goods or services or even experiences. It is the transformation of the customer.

A real expert understands that he has been hired to change people, in order to produce a better outcome. He is a catalyst for change, which starts with the way he listens.

A real expert practices what I call "transformational listening." Transformational listening goes beyond listening for data, information, or knowledge; it is listening for wisdom and insight. It goes beyond listening with the physical ears; it is listening with ears of discernment. Transformational listening is not a set of techniques; it is a way of being with another person. It is not based on some clever approach or device; it is based on the deep-down way we see others and ourselves.

An outstanding example of a true expert who practiced transformational listening in his work with clients and donors was Paul Laughlin. Paul was the bank trust officer in Hattiesburg, Mississippi, who turned a conversation with Osceola McCarty, a black 87-year-old washer woman, into a magnificent gift to the University of Southern Mississippi that completely re-defined philanthropy at that institution. Here's the inside story of her amazing donation.

[Personal note: I was a professor of business law at the University of Southern Mississippi in the mid-1980's and later was associated with the USM Foundation's Estate Planning Advisory Board. I was vice-president and trust officer at Trustmark National Bank in the late 1980's, where I was acquainted with some of the participants in these events.]

*In 1995, at the age of 87, Osceola McCarty had a problem. This simple, hardworking lady had saved and penny-pinched her way* *to an estate worth over $200,000 and she wasn't sure what to do with it. The tellers at Trustmark National Bank sent her to see Paul Laughlin, the bank's assistant vice-president and trust officer.*

*Listening to her story, Paul learned that Osceola had washed and ironed other people's clothes all her life until she "retired" at age 86 due to arthritis in her hands. She had never married and never had any children. Most of "her people" had passed away earlier, so she needed some advice on what to do with her life savings.*

*Paul, recognizing her lack of formal education, used a masterful approach to uncover her deeply-held passions. He took out 10 dimes and spread them on the coffee table in front of her. "Miss Osceola," he said, "show me with the dimes what you want to do with your money."*

*"Well," she began, picking up the first dime, "I've always believed in tithing, so this one's got to go to the church."*

*"And I've got two nieces and a nephew I want to help," she continued, picking up three more dimes. "These are for them." Then she hesitated.*

*"And what about the rest?" Paul queried.*

*She studied Paul as if to see if she could trust him, smiled nervously, took a deep breath, and said, "You know, I always wanted to be a teacher. But my auntie got sick when I was in the sixth grade, and she didn't have anybody to take care of her. I stopped going to school to tend her, and I was never able to go back. After she died, I was too far behind, so I just kept working, washing and ironing and saving my money. So I never got to be a teacher."*

*Her eyes filled with tears. She paused and looked away, then composed herself and went on.*

*"But I understand the college in town helps black kids become teachers. I want to help them."*

*"You mean the University of Southern Mississippi?" Paul asked. "Yes, that's the one," she replied. "What do you know about the University of Southern Mississippi, Miss Osceola?"*

*"Actually, I've never even seen the place. It's too far to walk and I never owned a car. But I understand they help black kids become teachers. I'm too old to do it myself, but I'd like to help some of them become teachers."*

Paul wisely recognized that she would have needs during the rest of her lifetime, so he helped her set up what we in the business would call a charitable remainder arrangement. The fund provided income to her during her lifetime, then went to the University of Southern Mississippi to pay for scholarships for black students in education.

Paul also realized that sometimes, the story about a gift can be more valuable than the gift itself. He got her permission to tell the University about her donation.

News of that gift hit the University of Southern Mississippi and the town of Hattiesburg like a Category Five hurricane. The whole community was electrified! A lot of people with a lot more money than Osceola McCarty looked at themselves and asked, *"Wow, if a black washerwoman can do something like that, what's wrong with me?"*

Long before she died and her $150,000 gift passed to the University, there were millions of dollars in the Osceola McCarty Scholarship Fund, helping to fund scholarships for needy black students in education. Her gift changed hundreds of lives.

It changed her life too. This humble little lady finally saw with her own eyes the University of Southern Mississippi, where they awarded her the first honorary degree in the history of the school. She saw the whole country. She saw the White House—from the inside, where President Clinton awarded her the Presidential Citizen's Medal and scores of other humanitarian honors. Harvard University awarded her an honorary doctorate and she won the United Nations' coveted Avicenna Medal for educational commitment.

Through it all, she retained her grace and humility. *"I can't do everything,"* she said, *"but I can do something to help somebody. And what I can do I will do. I wish I could do more."*

Looking beyond her age, her profession, her lack of education, the diminutive size of her banking account, and the color of her skin, Paul listened to Osceola and saw a vision for her future happiness and heard an opportunity to make a meaningful difference in the world. Only after applying his expertise as a listener did he deploy his expertise in estate planning and charitable giving.

As a result, Paul not only transformed Osceola's life but he also dramatically changed the lives of an entire university community, of dozens of future Mississippi school teachers, and of untold numbers of philanthropists and their advisors who have been inspired by this story. Generations yet unborn will be blessed by Paul's transformational listening.

> **Transformational listening is not a set of techniques; it is a way of being with another person. It is based on the deep-down way we see others and ourselves.**

If you were to talk with Paul, you would discover a man of great humility, respect, and curiosity. These attributes are essential for the transformational listener.

The transformational listener is **humble**. He sees himself as constantly open to new understanding. He knows that, as much as he already knows, he still has much to learn about the client's or donor's world. He understands that careful, attentive, and appreciative listening both with his ears and with his heart is the only way he will learn enough about their world to become an expert in it.

The transformational listener is **respectful**. Regardless of the apparent disparity in age, education, wealth, achievement, rank, status, or power, he sees clients or donors as fellow human travelers, each with unique experiences and exceptional brilliance. He acknowledges their strengths and talents, and honors their life journeys. He knows every person he meets has something important to teach him.

The transformational listener is **curious**. He can't wait to discover what lies within the clients' or donors' every phrase or paragraph or silent pause. He is fascinated by where their minds will go next, by what stories or insights will spring forth from their thinking if he listens generously and without interruption.

As Paul Laughlin showed, being a real expert is first about listening and only then about speaking. It is more about what we are presently learning than what we previously knew. It is more about harnessing shared brilliance than showing off as a solitary shooting star. It is more about a way of seeing others and being with people than the mastery of a set of techniques.

In the end, it is all about touching hearts and changing lives.

# the art of listening to stories

It goes without saying, but perhaps needs to be said anyway, that one who asks an authentic story-leading question must truly care about hearing the answer, wherever that answer may lead. An authentic story-leading question is not a technique but is the outward expression of a caring and curious heart.

I have discovered that successful Level-Two advisors manage five different threads of thought as clients or donors share their stories. That is, they simultaneously listen to the narrative in five unique but interrelated ways:

1) **Level-Two advisors listen for enjoyment.** That is, they listen for the pure pleasure of the story. They are intrigued with the thread of the story and the craft of the storyteller, and they are intensely curious to discover where the story and the storyteller will go next.

   They know that, like snowflakes, no two stories and no two storytellers are alike. They relish this diversity and take pleasure in the uniqueness of each story-sharing occasion.

   We see an example of this aspect of story listening on full display at socials or cocktail parties. Partiers entertain each other with their stories, and the most popular guests are those who tell the most captivating stories or who excel in story listening.

2)    **Level-Two advisors listen for facilitation.** They attend the client's or donor's storytelling for the purpose of aiding the flow of the narrative. They realize that every good storyteller requires the attention of a good story listener. This attention is evidenced by facial expressions, body language, verbalizations, and occasional questions to nudge the story along. These actions demonstrate that they are present with the story and the storyteller.

But good story listeners are also aware that the delivery of this attention must be played with a deft hand. They know that too much intrusion into the storytelling will crush the narrative, not support it. They are ever present, but never overwhelmingly so.

We see an example of this aspect of story listening when a good friend comes to share a difficult personal experience. With a reassuring air and gentle coaxing, we create a safe and inviting environment that helps them tell their story. We share the responsibility with them of unfolding the narrative, piece by piece.

3)    **Level-Two advisors listen for perspective.** They are aware that every story is told from some point of view, so they listen to stories in order to understand where their clients or donors are coming from.

Like CSI detectives who study the patterns of casings, bullet holes, and ricochets to calculate where the suspected shooter stood, story-listening advisors pay careful attention to the perspectives in their clients' and donors' stories and thus learn where their clients and donors see themselves in their families, in their communities, and in the world. In this way, advisors are able to empathize more fully and work more closely with their clients and donors.

We see an example of this aspect of story listening in mediation, where the mediator asks each side to recite its version of what happened. From those accounts, the mediator is able to recognize the point of view that each party brings to the table. Hopefully, with that insight, the mediator is able to help the parties appreciate and relate to everyone else's perspectives.

**4)**    **Level-Two advisors listen for messages or morals.** By their nature, nearly all stories have a point. When a story is used in a teaching situation, the lesson is often stated overtly. (Remember Aesop's Fables? "And the moral of this fable is . . . ")   When stories are used in conversation, most carry a moral or message, but that message is usually not spelled out. But by listening attentively, advisors can identify the morals in their clients' or donors' stories.

Recognizing the morals of clients' or donors' stories is a key to understanding their value system. Indeed, this is one of the most effective ways to discern client or donor values. The advisor who misses the point of his client's or donor's stories is usually in the dark about what they truly value.

We see this aspect of story listening when we attend a lecture or sermon and the speaker uses a story or parable as part of his argument. In that setting, we don't just listen passively to the story. Instead, as the narrative develops, our minds race ahead to see if we can identify the message the speaker intends. We feel a sense of satisfaction when we "get it," that is, when we understand the point the speaker is trying to make with the story.

**5)**    **Level-Two advisors listen for discernment.** They listen with what I call "the ears of the heart" and they find that they know things beyond what is contained in the stories.

Call it intuition, call it wisdom, call it the ability to put disparate pieces of the puzzle together—whatever you like, it leads to exceptional insight and understanding. This in turn leads to masterful counsel and life-changing planning. It creates an entirely new realm of professional value and it vaults the advisor and the client into a new dimension in their relationship.

We see this component of story listening when a troubled grandchild converses with a wise and patient grandparent. Based on years of experience, genuine affection, and an awareness of the uniqueness of the grandchild, the grandparent senses things not perceived by the casual observer. As a result, there is an added depth of communication and an increased height of understanding.

[
**Level Two requires the ability to work comfortably in the world of story; to engage artfully in the give and take of story sharing in a professional setting.**
]

When woven together, these five different listening-threads create a magic carpet for the clients' or donors' stories. Both the storyteller and the story listener are transported to an enchanted place: a place of wonder, a place of respect, a place of understanding, and a place of connection.

# using many different types of stories

The ability to craft and tell a wide variety of story-types is one of the key components of the skill-set needed to operate effectively at Level Two.

To the uninitiated, a reference to many different types of stories can be a little confusing. Before enlightenment, we tend to think of stories as a giant, monolithic, homogenous collection of narratives. But just as the Eskimo knows in his frigid world that there are many different kinds of snow, you discover once you drill down into the world of stories in professional and personal relationships that there are lots of different kinds of stories.

In his groundbreaking book, *The Leader's Guide to Storytelling: Mastering the Art and Discipline of Business Narrative,* Stephen Denning details the application of eight different styles of narrative, and references many others. Dr. Denning describes these eight story patterns and their purposes:

1)    Stories to motivate others to action: using narrative to ignite action and implement new ideas.

2)   Stories to build trust in you: using narrative to communicate who you are.

3)   Stories to build trust in your company: using narrative to build your brand.

4)   Stories to transmit your values: using narrative to instill organizational values.

5)   Stories to get others working together: using narrative to get things done collaboratively.

6)   Stories to share knowledge: using narrative to transmit knowledge and understanding.

7)   Stories to tame the grapevine: using narrative to neutralize gossip and rumor.

8)   Stories to create and share your vision: using narrative to lead people into the future.

In my third book, *Double Your Sales: An Honest and Authentic Approach to Professional Selling,* I show how to use a dozen different types of narrative in sequence to turn prospects into clients.

1)   The Banana/Lettuce Story: how to manage expectations for the engagement meeting.

2)   The New Me Story: how to introduce yourself and describe why you are different from your competitors.

3)   The Who Are You Story: how to understand prospects' backgrounds.

4)   The Worry Story: how to help prospects articulate their concerns.

5)   The Hidden Waterfall Story: how to communicate unseen or unacknowledged dangers to prospects.

6)   The Consequences Story: how to help prospects envision the possible ramifications of failing to properly address their problems.

7)   The Benefit Story: how to help prospects envision the possible positive outcomes of properly addressing their problems.

8)   The Kind of Like You Story: how to share a mini-testimonial from an earlier client or donor.

9)   The How We Do It Story: how to describe your process for addressing their worries and concerns.

10)  The Investment Story: how to create a context for understanding the way you charge for your products or services.
11)  The Dress Rehearsal Story: how to inoculate prospects against "buyer's remorse."
12)  The Next Step Story: how to describe where we go from here.

It is beyond the scope of this book to teach professional advisors how to use all these—and many other—different types of stories, or even to catalogue them all. The point of these lists from just two of the many books on the subject is to open your eyes to the vast array of narrative-types that exist, and to invite you to dive in to the exciting world of story.

Once you become aware of the possibilities, the next step is to identify a few story-types you want to learn to use more effectively. Read about them; understand how and why they work; learn the contexts in which they should and shouldn't be used; create your own versions of them; then practice, practice, practice.

Using a wide variety of stories in a professional context isn't rocket science, but it is an art or skill that requires attention, intention, and consistent application. It is, in my view, an essential skill for the successful Level-Two advisor.

# a new tool-set

Working effectively and efficiently in the rarified air of Level Two will require us to employ *a new tool-set*. Tools—whether simple tools like the wheel, the lever, or the inclined plane, or complex tools like the computer, the automobile, or the airplane—are devices that allow us to accomplish bigger results with less exertion, in less time, with less resistance, and/or at a lower cost than we could achieve working with our bare hands.

Given the huge expenditure of energy and attention required for most of us to transform ourselves and our practices from Level One to Level Two, we probably couldn't pull it off without a smart set of appropriate tools, custom-designed for the task. We would simply wear out before we arrived or would get lost along the way.

A large part of my journey during the past 15 or so years has been to design, test, hone, and refine a set of story-based tools for the professional advisor seeking to move to Level Two and Level Three. One of the things I learned along the way is that there are different phases of a client or donor relationship, and these different phases often require different tools. In evaluating tools that they might choose to use in their own practice, professional advisors must pay attention to the phase or phases in which those tools will be applied.

Here is what I call **"The Five Phases of Client or Donor Relationships:"**

**Phase One: The Attraction Phase.** In this phase, we are seeking to get noticed in a positive way by potential customers or donors. Of necessity we must cast a broad net, because we don't know precisely who will hear our message and respond to it. Think of this as marketing, public relations, and all that goes with those efforts.

**Phase Two: The Engagement Phase.** In this phase, someone has responded to our attraction efforts and now we get to discover if we will both choose to work together. Now we get up close and personal. Think of this as sales, turning a prospect into a client or donor who has decided to move forward.

**Phase Three: The Service Phase.** In this phase, we have agreed to work together. We have a client or donor, and we must provide the services our organization promises to deliver. This phase could be brief or very long, depending on our business model.

**Phase Four: The Retention Phase.** In this phase, we work to maintain and perhaps deepen our ongoing relationship with the client or donor. We strive to find ways to deliver continuing value and thus receive recurring revenue from the relationship. We recognize that it's a lot easier and less expensive to retain a customer than to develop a new one.

**Phase Five: The Multigenerational Engagement Phase.** In this phase, we extend our relationships with clients and donors up and down their family trees and out into the branches. We see parents and grandparents, children and grandchildren, aunts, uncles, and cousins as a logical extension of our services. We look for ways to have a clan-wide circle of influence and relationship.

# a new set of story-based tools

In the realm of legacy building, there are lots of tools around. Many are very beautiful, some are rather clever, and a few are quite expensive. Unfortunately, nearly all of them are largely impractical.

Most clients don't have the time or the ability to sit down and write their life story. Most clients aren't inclined to produce a feature film about their lives, or to bankroll a lavish family legacy retreat. They want the process of sharing the meaning of their lives and the wholeness of their wealth to be simple and practical and fun. They want it to fit in with the rest of their life.

Over the past 15 years or so, I have created and gathered a collection of story-based tools to help financial advisors, estate planners, and philanthropic professionals succeed in this role. These tools are practical, fun, easy-to-use, and effective. They are elegant yet simple. They fit seamlessly within a busy practice. They actually work with real clients and real advisors.

The SunBridge model offers a number of tools to attract, establish, strengthen, and maintain Level-Two client relationships. These tools apply the power of story to draw people in and touch their hearts, whether one-to-one or in a group.

With these tools, professional advisors can connect deeply and quickly with donors, clients, and prospects, and help them build a legacy of significance. Professional advisors can become the most trusted and admired advisor, the one to whom clients and donors bring their donations, their business, and their referrals. These tools make it easier for professional advisors to infuse new meaning and energy into their clients' and donors' lives, which produces the same in the advisors' work.

# a unique set of conceptual tools

Some of the SunBridge conceptual tools have been introduced earlier in this book. These include:

**The Client Service Gap.** This is a conceptual tool to help advisors understand how their current offerings compare to what clients and donors say they most want from their advisors.

**The Life Circle.** This is a conceptual tool that teaches the breadth and interrelatedness of our wealth, shows the major elements of our lives and relationships, and illustrates the importance of our values, stories, and life-vision.

**The Legacy Circle.** This is a conceptual model that identifies the key components of a legacy filled with passion and purpose, and outlines how the various components should fit together.

**Taking Charge.** This is a conceptual tool that clarifies the four-step process required for us to make real and lasting change, when we decide to take charge of our daily habits.

Besides the conceptual tools, SunBridge offers three additional groups of tools for the Level-Two Advisor's toolbox. First, there is a significant group of presentation tools for teaching and introducing these principles to audiences small and large. Second, one of the most important groups is the Priceless Conversation family of tools for creating brief but deeply meaningful story-based interviews. Third, there is an additional cluster of tools for working directly with clients and donors on a one-to-one or one-to-two basis.

# a unique set of presentation tools

SunBridge teaches a different philosophy from most when it comes to the purposes for giving a professional marketing presentation and how to achieve those purposes. We believe that there are two primary objectives when making a professional marketing presentation: 1) to connect on a human-to-human level with members of the audience; and 2) to make it as easy as possible to move to a one-to-one meeting with those who are interested in your message, where the possibility of working together can be explored. Everything else is secondary to those two aims.

> **There are two primary objectives when making a professional marketing presentation: to connect on a human to human level and to move to a one-on-one meeting.**

We believe the best way to connect on a human level is through stories. In a presentation, we teach best by telling stories and we connect best by listening attentively to other's stories. There is an art, I believe, to asking story-leading questions to the audience while leading a presentation and to listening attentively to their answers while standing in front of an audience.

All the presentation tools in the SunBridge toolbox are built on this premise: teach by telling your stories, connect by getting the audience to share theirs. Here's a summary of some of the main ones:

- **Building Bridges**
  This is a powerfully emotional presentation involving lecture content and on-screen visuals to examine how all of us are bridge builders of one sort or another. It challenges the audience to take an honest look at the bridges they're building, and how their life will affect others. It explores how we can leave a legacy using all of our wealth—both financial and non-financial—to tell the story that will be left when we are gone.

- **Building Bridges: The Philanthropic Power of the Legacy Story**
  This variation of the Building Bridges presentation invites donors to realize that the bridges they build will ultimately determine the stories that will be told about them. Through examples of others who made a difference by giving from the heart, they learn that we can all matter, regardless of how much or how little we think we have to share.

- **Stories, Pictures & Heirlooms: Bequests from the Heart**
  This presentation creates human-to-human connection between the presenter and the members of the audience by tapping into the experiences and feelings associated with our stories, family pictures, and heirlooms. Attendees are invited to bring two or three photos from their personal history, plus a family heirloom. During the presentation, they share some of their most meaningful stories, and are taught how to combine stories with pictures and heirlooms to enhance the value of both, as well as how to preserve and pass on their stories, pictures, and heirlooms to future generations.

- **My Life in a Brown Paper Bag**
  This interactive presentation uses a simple concept to create a profound experience. Participants bring three items that have special meaning for them in a brown paper bag, and share with the other participants what makes these items so meaningful. This program facilitates the discovery of each other's deepest self and the discovery of what really makes us tick, through the use of small personal objects and the stories behind them. The result is deep connection and significant personal insights.

- **The Lighthouse**
  This is a presentation for a charitable organization, church group, service club, or similar setting, based on the "Turning Points" video and closely tied to the Life Circle. Simple and powerful, it helps us see the potential impact of the small acts—and the small objects—in our lives and the lives of others. Questions asked during the presentation include, "What was one of the best gifts anyone ever gave you?" and "What's one of most important lessons anyone ever taught you?"

- **Living Legacy: Words from the Heart**
No one likes to address the issue of how we will be remembered after we die, but it need not be somber or unsettling. This presentation for groups of 8-16 people is designed to help participants approach this important issue in a thoughtful and comfortable way, and to see and appreciate their legacy as a passing on of the wealth of their life's meaning, and not just their material assets. This program demonstrates the power of words of wisdom left to children and grandchildren by a parent or ancestor and can serve as an introduction to a Priceless Conversation or a Personal Legacy Declaration.

- **The Treasure Chest**
This presentation uses a group game to create sharing and deeper introspection, helping participants recognize the wisdom in all of us. It's easy and fun to develop a warm, uplifting experience with any group during client or donor meetings, family reunions, and office retreats, using a set of "wooden nickel" tokens tucked inside a real wood "treasure chest" or a cloth drawstring "booty bag."

- **I Come from a People**
This is a group introductory exercise that promotes a depth of connection in a few minutes while allowing participants to connect with and share their heritage and their most important values. In place of stale and trite group introductions ("Hi, my name is John and I'm an accountant."), this creates an almost immediate sense of belonging and connection on a rich and meaningful human level.

- **Fire & Water**
This is a storytelling exercise that gets clients and donors involved in sharing memories of experiences with fire and water. Deep connections and profound insights into the client's values often emerge from memories the client or donor has about these two elements.

- **Priceless Objects, Important Stories**
  This is a small group activity that explores the true value of important objects that will become part of the clients' legacy if the bonds between the objects and their associated stories are unbroken. It motivates clients and donors to consider the real value of their tangible personal effects.

# a unique set of interview tools: priceless conversations

Priceless Conversation interviews are the perfect tools for SunBridge advisors to conduct brief but deeply meaningful story-based conversations with their clients and donors about the issues that are most on their minds and in their hearts. They allow them to share the stories and life-wisdom that most define who they really are and what they most want to convey to those they love. They help SunBridge advisors to create richly significant and appropriate plans for them and to offer more appropriate counsel.

Each of the nearly 40 different Priceless Conversations available to SunBridge advisors comes in a complete tool kit. Each kit includes an introductory booklet, a questions booklet, a CD personalized with the client's name in a black leatherette CD case. All of this is packaged in a handsome black gift box and beautifully wrapped with a ribbon ready to present to the client. Here is a summary of the many varieties of Priceless Conversations.

- **Priceless Conversations: legacy**
  Life's Greatest Treasures Your real wealth is the living declaration of who you are as a unique human being, of the path you have traveled in your life, and the bridge of values, vision, wisdom, and experience that you have to offer. Pass on this true wealth in your own words.

> **Priceless Conversations are the perfect tools to conduct a deeply meaningful story-based interview about the most important issues on their minds and in their hearts.**

- **Priceless Conversations: the meaning of money**
  Using Wealth Wisely — Don't just leave them money; leave them your life-lessons about how to use money with skill and judgment. Discover within yourself a treasure house of wisdom about the meaning of money—wisdom that will guide them to place true value on what they own.

- **Priceless Conversations: wisdom**
  A Record of Wisdom and Values — Wisdom is something personal, unique to you alone, a kind of wealth that, like all wealth, can be shared and passed along to those you love. Don't let it remain buried alive within you, but let it be dusted off, cherished, and remembered for generations to come.

- **Priceless Conversations: the meaning of success**
  A Guide to Successful Living — Explore and share your learning of what it means and what it takes to achieve success in life: professional success; educational success; financial success; success in relationships; and personal success. Your wisdom and insights can be a stepping stone to their success.

- **Priceless Conversations: my values**
- **Priceless Conversations: our family values**
  A Legacy of Value and Virtue —You've learned that it's not hard to make good decisions when you know what your values are. Now you can share those values and teach those you love the joys of a values-centered, purpose-filled life. Surely there can be no greater mission for your life.

- **Priceless Conversations: my baby**
  A Parent's Love — A new baby is like the beginning of all things - wonder, hope, a dream of possibilities. It is vitally important for the new parent to express some of the almost inexpressible feelings he or she has for this infant and the experience of becoming a mother or father.

- **Priceless Conversations: children**
  Words of Love and Protection — Capture your fondest wishes for your children's happiness, especially if you pass away before they grow up. Share your hopes, dreams, and instructions for them and those who will guide their footsteps in your absence. Your love can shelter them from life's storms.

- **Priceless Conversations: our special child**
  Sheltering a Precious Lamb — Your special child, with their unique gifts and challenges, will need your love and understanding all their life, even after you're gone. Share your caring and your insights with your special child and with those who will shepherd them when you're not here.

- **Priceless Conversations: an angel remembered**
  Keeping Their Memory Alive — Your child will always be a part of you, regardless of what else may happen in your life. Preserve the memories and stories of the precious spirit too soon taken away; recall the laughter and the tears they brought into the world, so that they can never be forgotten.

- **Priceless Conversations: childhood years**
  Capturing Our Children's Stories — Children ages 6-12 grow up so quickly that memories of their insight, honesty, and youthful exuberance can easily be lost. This special process of annual interviews will keep alive the memories of this special but fleeting time of life.

- **Priceless Conversations: adult children**
  Ties That Bind Forever — One season follows another, laden with happiness and tears, and before we know it, our little ones are grown with little ones of their own. We must tell them that we love them, and why, for we are bound together forever.

- **Priceless Conversations: grandchildren**
  Generations of Love — There's a special bond that seems to leapfrog generations, connecting young and old in the magic of family ties. Your words of wisdom and the sound of your voice can be a beacon, an anchor, and a harbor safe from the gales of life.

- **Priceless Conversations: love**
  Adventures of our Life Together — When you love them, you need to tell them. And when they're the love of your life, it's important to capture those feeling and those expressions as a permanent reminder of how much you cherish the life you've built together. When love is shared, it grows.

- **Priceless Conversations: my Christian faith**
- **Priceless Conversations: my Jewish faith**
- **Priceless Conversations: my Catholic faith**
- **Priceless Conversations: my LDS faith**
- **Priceless Conversations: my spirituality**
  Yearnings of the Soul — Spiritual values go to the very essence of who we are as human being and who we are as a people. The story of our faith or spiritual journey is an epic account that needs to be told and re-told to current and future generations.

- **Priceless Conversations: my house**
  Home is Where the Heart Is — The places you've lived hold some of your most enjoyable stories and lessons. Revisit the homes of your past and you will strike a mother lode of memories, a rich vein of experiences that can be mined for a deeper meaning and understanding of your life.

- **Priceless Conversations: alma mater**

  An Education for Life — We feel a soul-deep allegiance toward our schools. They shaped and molded us, and prepared us for a life of meaning and purpose. They affected the way we see the world and the way we ourselves. Now we can share cherished memories and our feeling of connection to our alma mater.

- **Priceless Conversations: sharing**

  Generosity that Matters — Giving back, through generosity and serving others, makes our lives richer and more meaningful. Telling others the purposes behind our generosity and the experiences that motivate our giving strengthen and encourage those who come behind us to give more and serve more, and in the process, to discover their own life purpose.

- **Priceless Conversations: giving (for nonprofit organizations)**

  Generosity that Matters — Whether we give publicly or in private, it is important to share with others the purposes and passion behind our giving, so that our commitment to the causes and organization we benefit may evolve into a perpetual monument to the human spirit. Without the stories behind the gifts, important lessons are lost to future generations.

- **Priceless Conversations: pets**

  Man's Best Friends — The friendship, loyalty, and companionship of pets are exquisite treasures to be cherished and remembered. You need to recall how they have touched your life, to give instructions for their care, and to share your insights about their larger role in our lives.

- **Priceless Conversations: my plan**
- **Priceless Conversations: our plan (for couples)**

  Protecting and Providing for Those I/We Love — There are many reasons for doing estate planning, but ultimately they all boil down to this: we want to touch the hearts and lives of those we love, even in our absence. In this process, we can share what our lives have meant and what we hope for the lives of others.

- **Priceless Conversations: angels and heroes**
  Lives That Touch Our Hearts — Your life has been lifted and enriched by the people who befriended you, took you under their wing, and went out of their way to help you along life's journey. As you tell their stories and how they made a difference for you, you also share important understanding about your own life.

- **Priceless Conversations: turning points**
  The Hinges of Our Lives — Looking back at the significant moments of your life and relating how those events have helped to shape the person you have become, the deeper meaning of your life comes into clearer focus. The narrative of your journey is a rich and intriguing tapestry that will touch others' lives for good.

- **Priceless Conversations: treasures**
  Possessions of Deep Emotional Value — By caring for your precious keepsakes and documenting their stories, you give three priceless gifts: the treasures themselves, your dedication in preserving them and their meaning, and a richer understanding of your life and your family's history.

- **Priceless Conversations: tribute**
  They Touched Our Lives for Good — Before they passed, they were heroes who lived for something bigger than themselves. While they lived, they touched the hearts and changed the lives of those around them. We must now preserve their stories so they are never forgotten.

- **Priceless Conversations: wishes**
  Honoring Our Later Years — Making the last chapters of your life meaningful and truly reflective of your values can sometimes be challenging. It requires that you take steps now to explain and document how you want others to implement what you have decided concerning your care.

- **Priceless Conversations: veteran**

  The Legacy of Heroes — "The secret of Happiness is Freedom, and the secret of Freedom, Courage." (Thucydides) Veterans' stories of courage in defense of our freedoms must not be lost. Their stories must be heard, shared, and saved, lest we forget the price they paid to allow us to enjoy life, liberty, and the pursuit of happiness.

- **Priceless Conversations: year in review**

  Stories of a Year Gone By — The sands of time pass quickly through the hourglass of our lives, and without an occasion for pausing and reflecting on the meaning of the last twelve months, many of the rich blessings and important lessons of our life can be overlooked.

- **Priceless Conversations: my business**

  Creating Concrete Value — Building a successful business is one of the most challenging and underappreciated achievements of our time. The epic journey of creating concrete value for customers, employees, and family members is a story that needs to be told.

- **Priceless Conversations: celebrations**

  Occasions to Rejoice — Celebrations connect us as couples, as families, as communities, as religious groups, as nations, and as mankind. We need to share and preserve our memories of holidays, birthdays, anniversaries, gatherings, traditions, and milestones.

# a unique set of one-to-one tools

Once Level-Two advisors sit down one to one and start to plan with their clients or donors, they need special tools to engage them at a meaningful level. SunBridge provides an interesting array of these too. Here are some of them.

- **Personal Legacy Declaration Questionnaire**
  This booklet simplifies the process of creating a first draft of "words from the heart" and sharing wisdom with those we love. By answering a series of thoughtful questions, clients and donors provide the advisor with the raw material to start crafting a powerful and touching written document, similar to an "ethical will," but touching all the quadrants of the Life Circle and the Legacy Circle. The draft is then delivered back to the client or donor for further personalization.

- **Angels & Heroes**
  With the use of a visual time line, this tools helps clients and donors identify personalities who played a memorable role in their life as an "angel" or "hero"—someone who was exceptionally supportive, encouraging, or helpful to the client along the way. This one-to-one or small group activity creates a true and unvarnished view of a person's deepest and most closely held values by sharing the clients' or donors' stories of the most impactful people in their lives.

- **Lifeline of Significance**
  Similar to "Angels & Heroes," this tool uses a visual time line for identifying pivotal events in the client's life. This process helps both client and advisor get an overview of the client's history, and identify themes and trends in the way the client sees himself. From this one-to-one or small group activity, you get a thumbnail sketch of the major events of a lifetime that deepen understanding of the person and how they deal with life transitions.

- **The Oral Autobiography**
  This is a survey comprising hundreds of "universal story-leading questions" covering many areas and stages of experience from childhood through midlife and later. It gives the advisor a full profile of the client's history as seen by the client. It also captures the client's or donor's recollections of previous family history and their vision for the future.

- **The Bridge Builder**

  This is a powerful piece about the importance of serving, giving back, and leaving a legacy for those who come after us. This timeless classic in poetry conveys a clear and unmistakable message to clients and donors that life's greatest joys come from paying it forward.

- **The Book of Life**

  This simple tool elegantly solves a vexing and complex problem: how to capture and organize the myriad of stories and experiences that make up our life history, in a way that is both fun and effective. Once clients and donors see it, they get it and can't wait to get started cataloguing their own lessons and narratives.

- **My Life, My Legacy**

  This handsome leather binder and the exercises inside it unfold the quadrants and major components of the Life Circle into a comprehensive summary of the life-wisdom of clients and donors for their loved ones. The result is a clear statement of all aspects of the client's or donor's life and legacy.

- **How Will You Be Remembered?**

  Used in conjunction with a probing essay with the same title, this 11x17 worksheet tool helps clients and donors clarify the difference they want to make in each of the key roles and relationships of their lives. It then guides them on how to get started to purposefully create the legacy they will leave in each role or relationship.

- **Building Your Legacy with Passion & Purpose**

  This 11x17 worksheet tool empowers advisors and clients to find what matters most in each component of the client's legacy and then create a game plan for making it happen.

- **Memorandum of Significant Personal Property**
  This is an estate planning tool designed not only to designate who is to receive what, but also why the object is significant, why each recipient was chosen to receive it, and what they will hopefully do with it upon receipt.

# a new support-set

Equipped with a new mind-set, a new skill-set, and a new tool-set, aspiring Level-Two advisors need one more thing to effect lasting change. Given our human tendencies to slip back into old patterns, fall back into old habits, or run out of resolve, we will need *a new support-set* in order to complete this transformation.

We need scaffolding to prop us up and an outside push to keep us moving forward as we embrace this new approach to life and work. We need goals and deadlines and accountability. We need pioneers who have blazed the trail ahead and guides and outfitters for the journey. We need coaches and teammates and cheerleaders and more-experienced players as role-models.

Hopefully, we can develop a community of like-minded colleagues who are on the same journey, a circle of friends who share our vision and who are willing to help us as we help them. In this case, it really does take a village. At SunBridge, that village is called the SunBridge Legacy Builder Network. Whether you participate in that group or some other organization, it is essential to your long-term transformation to surround yourself with plenty of support.

[
Given our human tendencies to slip back into old
patterns or lose our resolve, we need a new support-set in
order to effect lasting change.
]

# the story-based initial meeting

Mr. Jacobs's story and the story of Paul Laughlin's work with Osceola McCarty are wonderful examples of how listening to the client or donor can lead to a level of service that reaches far beyond the limited thinking and vision of Level One. Story is the key to Level-Two relationships, and there's no better place to start than the initial client meeting.

The story-based initial meeting involves at least five steps:

1) The Story of Who You Are
2) The Story of Who the Client Is
3) The Story of the Client's Worries, Concerns, Hopes and Dreams
4) The Story of Your Process
5) The Story of What the Client Understood

**The Story of Who You Are** – In this step, you briefly tell the client or donor in narrative form about yourself and the way you practice. This should include sharing, in simple terms, your commitment to wealth as more than money and property, and the emphasis you place on working with clients as human beings rather than just a bunch of facts and figures. Then, invite him to tell you a little about himself.

**The Story of Who The Client Is** – Switching from presenter to audience, you now encourage the client or donor to tell you about his life, values, and whether or not there's a particular situation that prompted his coming to see you. Some clients may find it daunting to begin talking to you about what's on their mind, but by asking a few encouraging, story-leading questions, you can easily help them past this. Remember, telling our stories is natural; we all want to be heard, understood, and appreciated.

**The Story of the Client's Worries, Concerns, Hopes and Dreams** – Once the client or donor has shared some of his story with you; you naturally want to move to the substantive concerns that led him to agree to meet with you. You look to see if his worries, concerns, hopes, and dreams coincide with your areas of expertise. You explore whether he can vividly picture both the consequences of failing to address his concerns and the benefits of working together to address them, in order to determine if the solutions you can offer him are worth the cost of implementing them.

**The Story of Your Process** – Your narrative of how you help clients and donors address their concerns and realize their hopes and dreams is a powerful part of the sequence of turning prospects into clients and donors. It says you are experienced, you are thorough, you are reliable, and you are concerned about achieving great results. As you tell this "how we do it" story, the client or donor becomes more comfortable and confident in working with you.

**The Story of What the Client Understood** – In this last step, again ask the client if there are questions. Then, after answering any questions to the client's satisfaction, ask: "If you were going to tell someone later today about this meeting and what we accomplished, what would you say?" You then gently coach the client in restating the benefits of working with you that he discovered during the meeting. The purpose of this step is to make sure that the client is clear, before leaving, about these benefits.

More detailed instructions on how to create a powerful and effective story-based initial meeting can be found in my book *Double Your Sales: An Honest and Authentic Approach to Professional Selling,* and the associated website *DoubleYourSalesNow.com.* In that book, you will learn that relationship-building is the chief aim of the story-based initial meeting. Building a relationship with the client or donor depends on your ability to focus on understanding his or her needs and concerns, *and your willingness to listen rather than talk about your products and services.*

The best way to build a relationship and understand a client's needs and concerns is through stories. As clients tell you their story, they come to understand their needs, concerns, and values better themselves. Because they see that you share this understanding, they become receptive to the solutions you have to offer.

*What the client says to you is far more important than what you say to the client.* Most professionals are accustomed to "selling by telling." Telling is easy, but ineffective. The best way to persuade is not to persuade. Ask questions, listen, understand, and acknowledge, then your clients will become receptive to your solutions themselves.

# marketing at level two

A large segment of today's consumer population responds far more favorably to a "high-touch" rather than "high-tech" approach. They want to work with consultants who have the same values they do, who believe in socially responsible investing and giving, who are just as comfortable talking about feelings as ideas, and who can understand that this value extends beyond money and property alone. These clients are seeking to lead a meaningful life; the consultant who can meet them on common ground will be in an ideal position to establish a richly rewarding, potentially lifelong relationship with them.

We go into considerable depth in the SunBridge workshops about how to market a Level-Two practice. In this book, we can provide you with an overview to get you heading in the right direction. Success in establishing yourself as a Level-Two advisor obviously depends on creating Level-Two relationships in your practice. In the workshops, we focus on four areas:

**Building a Professional Referral Network** – Through your referral network, you'll work collaboratively with fellow advisors in other specialty areas who share your vision of client service, and recognize the abiding value of building relationships rather than simply carrying out transactions. By taking the time to listen to and share stories with fellow advisors, just as you've done with clients, you discover that there's much more to your professional relationships with your colleagues than just helping each other make money.

**Building a Personal Referral Network** – Clients who have experienced the power and scope of Level-Two advising are an excellent source of introductions to friends, relatives, and organizations. These clients typically are excited about sharing what they've discovered working with you. Here, you help them find ways to share this with others.

**Making Presentations** – When you're marketing as a Level-Two advisor, any presentation you make becomes a demonstration of the power of story, and of your commitment to financial advising as a process that serves the client as a whole person. Consequently, you will see your presentations creating human-to-human connections rather than merely conveying technical information. This requires that your presentations are structured not only so you can share one or more relevant stories, but also to give you the opportunity to listen to stories from your audience.

[
**Story is the key to Level-Two relationships, and there's no better place to start than the initial client meeting.**
]

**Collaborative Relationships Between Financial & Estate Advisors and Philanthropic Organizations** – This rich area of marketing involves a transformation of the reasons for giving that translates fundraising into philanthropy. In other words, it guides the charitable or philanthropic organization from Level-One to Level-Two thinking, with all the attendant benefits.

Everything about charitable giving changes for the better when both the advisor and the charity are focused on discovering the passions of the clients/donors and then bringing them together with those organizations that have missions consistent with the clients'/ donors' dreams, vision, and purpose. Donors stop feeling that they are being pursued and that giving is about getting a monkey off their backs. Instead, giving becomes an expression of their deepest values and an outlet for their biggest aspirations.

Level-Two collaboration between advisors and charities is a win-win equation: On one hand, the advisor directs clients to those organizations that can be an outlet for expressing their vision of their life's meaning and purpose; on the other, charitable organizations speak to prospective contributors as more than just potential dollars, which will allow them not only to reach these contributors but also to move them to action. Consequently, the size and scope of charitable gifts increases geometrically.

* * *

Your colleagues who are now Level-Two advisors will tell you that the use of story—in the telling and the listening—has breathed new life into the way they do business. It also transforms marketing from what may have become a lifeless and repetitive routine into a venue for enthusiasm, real sharing, and the discovery of prospects and clients as living, breathing, three-dimensional people who may be waiting for someone just like you to help them understand and appreciate just how wealthy they really are.

# SECTION 3

# client & advisor in the real world: level three

*"If you have built castles in the air, your work need not be lost; that is where they should be. Now put foundations under them."*

—Henry David Thoreau

## the transition from level two

f Level-One service is a line, and Level Two, a circle, then Level Three is a sphere. As we've seen, Level Two replaces the linear, transaction-thinking of Level One with the far richer element of the client's story. This allows you to have a much more human view of the client, which in turn means that you can be much more useful, and provide far greater value than you can at Level One—simply by listening and responding to the situations, values, concerns, needs, and desires expressed by the client's stories.

Shifting to Level Three ups the ante again. And it's crucial to understand that you can't just sit down with a client or donor and launch into a Level-Three conversation. *Level-Three advising arises out of a solid Level-Two relationship with a client or donor who's determined to live life deliberately, and take charge of his or her future.*

At Level Two, using the tools of story, you learned something about who the client is so you could respond meaningfully to situational concerns and problems. At Level Three, you'll use all the tools you've learned and practiced at Levels One and Two, but the context again expands, this time to include a vision of the client's cumulative past and future as a story in progress. Understanding this overarching story will allow you to respond not only to who the client is, but also to what this unique identity implies for the future—including the future of the client's business, family relationships, life in general—possibly even the future that extends far beyond the client's lifetime.

Then, as you'll see, your role will be to take this more or less theoretical vision of the client's life-story-into-the-future and translate it into action steps and timetables. **At Level Three, you become an architect who helps clients and donors design the future they want to live in.** You become the drafter of the blueprint that clarifies that vision and commits it to paper. You may also become the general contractor who takes those blueprints and helps clients and donors turn their visions into reality.

Just as we saw with the transformation into becoming a Level-Two advisor, the transformation into becoming a Level-Three advisor is not an instantaneous event but is an ongoing process. It too requires the persistent application and re-application of the same four essential ingredients: 1) a new mind-set; 2) a new skill-set; 3) a new tool-set; and 4) a new support-set. It too can create wonderful rewards for advisors and their clients and donors.

# level three is for master planners

Not every advisor is cut out to work at Level Three. Level-Three Planning is certainly not for the apprentice planner. Apprentice planners are still learning the ropes. They're trying to get all the rules, regulations, techniques, and explanations down. They are self-conscious and sometimes insecure. They worry about being "found out" as a neophyte. Generally, with sufficient time and experience, they'll progress to journeyman status.

Journeyman planners have passed through the learning curve. They know the ropes; they've learned the rules, regulations, techniques, and explanations. They keep up to date with current developments and they produce good plans. Their work product and their work style are completely adequate.

Most advisors with a few years of experience move from apprentice status into the journeyman category. But most never move beyond being a journeyman. Only a few become what I call "Master Planners." It is Master Planners who function comfortably and confidently at Level Three.

What distinguishes Master Planners from experienced, solid journeyman planners who never blossom into Master Planners?

Master Planners have wonderful command of planning tools and techniques, but so do many experienced journeyman planners. They tend to have many years of experience, but the same is true for others who have not achieved Master Planner status, and perhaps never will. They enjoy their work, but so do apprentices and journeymen. These are not what set this elite group apart.

[
**At Level Three, you become an
architect who helps clients and donors
design the future they want to live in.**
]

# three unique abilities, five profound principles

Master Planners possess three unique abilities and they understand and apply five profound principles. Some journeyman planners have some of these skills but not all of them or not much of them. It is this rare combination of talents and principles, blended in graceful harmony, that produces Master Planners, true Level-Three planners.

First, Master Planners have the ability to connect quickly and deeply with clients and donors. They can sit down in a business context with someone they've never met and within five minutes the client or donor is pouring out their heart to them. The client or donor feels an almost immediate sense of trust and understanding. The client or donor feels that they are truly being heard, perhaps for the first time by a planning professional. Because of this ability, Master Planners learn more about their clients and donors than journeyman planners ever do.

Second, Master Planners have the ability to see the future. I'm not talking about crystal balls and tarot cards. I'm referring to the Master Planner's gift for taking in a family situation, the current state of planning, a business or set of assets, and combining that information with their understanding of human nature and family dynamics, and knowing, literally knowing, how that scenario will ultimately play out. It's not that they've seen it before—often they have not—but they perceive things their journeyman colleagues do not, and they identify as significant certain human details that lesser planners gloss over. With that clear view of the future, they are ready to move forward.

Third, Master Planners create structures and processes that change the course of the future for their clients, and their families or businesses, or for their donors and the causes they champion. Having seen the future, they are prepared to re-write it. They understand the levers of transformation and how to pull them so that outcomes many months and years down the road are changed for the better. They "get" how legal, financial, philanthropic, and business tools and techniques operate in the real world with real people. As a result, they orchestrate elegant and effective solutions that work today and well into the future. Their plans are indeed masterpieces, works of art.

In addition to these three unique abilities, Master Planners understand five critical and powerful principles and how to apply them in their work.

Master Planners understand that, above all, they deliver wisdom. In a world awash with data and in the era of the "information superhighway" and the "knowledge worker," Master Planners recognize, in the words of Proverbs, that wisdom is more precious than rubies. They know that wisdom, the ability to apply knowledge and information with discernment and discretion, is that which sets them apart and for which they should be most abundantly compensated. They structure their business so they are in fact rewarded for their wisdom.

Master Planners understand that they operate in the fifth economy, the transformation economy. They know they are in the business of changing lives. They do not deal primarily in commodities, goods, services, or even experiences, although these are necessarily ingredients of what they do. Master Planners understand that, however their task has been described; they have in fact been hired to be a catalyst for changing people and producing lasting human improvements. Their professional offerings are presented so as to reflect this significant insight.

Master Planners understand that their most important professional skill is the ability to listen. They practice—or perhaps better said, they embody— transformational listening. Transformational listening goes beyond listening with the physical ears; it is listening with ears of discernment. Transformational listening is not a set of techniques; it is *a way of being* with another person. It is not based on some clever approach or device; it is based on the deep-down way Master Planners see themselves and others.

Master Planners understand the art of planning as well as the science. Like Fred Astaire or Michael Jackson, once they learn to count and they learn the steps, Master Planners begin to feel the rhythm of planning in their bones. They know instinctively how to move to the music. They have a sense of how things could be done that goes beyond what others taught them.   They take their craft beyond great to amazing.

Master Planners understand that collaboration is essential to their success. Regardless of the skill of the solo violinist, the greatest symphonic composition in the world is incomplete and unfulfilling without the rest of the orchestra. Master Planners are team players, not prima donnas. They are so comfortable in their own roles that they are neither jealous of nor intimidated by the talents of others. They enjoy bringing other world-class talent to the stage for the benefit of their clients and donors.

This rare combination—three unique abilities together with five profound understandings—is the constellation that produces Master Planners. When the stars align in this way, the result for clients and donors is planning that addresses the deepest and most significant issues in their lives and hearts. It addresses their deepest fears and worries and brings into reality their most important hopes and dreams.

For Master Planners, the result is the rare joy and fulfillment from comes from discovering the gifts that make them come alive and then employing those gifts to serve mankind. It is doing what they were put on this earth to do. For them, working at Level Three feels completely comfortable and natural.

# building a level-three practice

Keeping in mind what is required to become a Master Planner, let's examine what it takes to build a Level-Three practice. First we must clarify what the advisor delivers to the client or donor at Level Three.

In Section 1, as you'll recall, the Client Service Gap revealed to us the Flatland world of traditional financial advising. The top line of the chart, which presents the values that many clients and donors are seeking in their advisors, included the words *Connection, Significance, Vision, Wisdom,* and *Trust,* which we defined as follows:

**Connection** – Signifies an ongoing relationship based on intimate knowledge and understanding, developing into a deep and lasting friendship.

**Significance** – A sense of what matters most to the client or donor, a grasp of him or her as a human being whose life has meaning and purpose. A profound understanding of the client's or donor's life and experiences.

**Vision** – A far-reaching sense of what the client's or donor's life can be, and even wants to be. This may span generations in a family, family business, etc.

**Wisdom** – The ability to know what matters and what doesn't; to apply this knowledge by helping clients and donors see the significance of their lives, and unlock their potential to live more richly and fully in every sense.

**Trust** – Confidence that the advisor truly understands the client or donor and what matters most to him or her, and is deeply committed to putting the client's or donor's long-term well-being and fulfillment ahead of the advisor's.

[
**Level-Three advising arises out of a solid Level-Two relationship with a client or donor who's determined to live life deliberately, and take charge of his or her future.**
]

At Level Three, the advisor discerns the client's or donor's *mission* in life, and facilitates the fulfillment of that mission through a cluster of tangible services, *for which the client pays*. In the SunBridge model, this cluster of services is known as the "Level-Three Endowment."

Experienced advisors who have not been trained in the SunBridge method often tell me that they're already providing their clients with many of these things. I acknowledge that they probably are, but then I ask if their clients recognize, appreciate, and *pay* for them. Usually these seasoned advisors reply that, while some clients may recognize and appreciate them, they certainly aren't paying for them.

These advisors get paid instead for transactions, numbers, techniques, information, and advice—in short, the inventory that appears at the bottom of the Client Service Gap illustration. Like many of their colleagues, these so-called "bottom-line" advisors are charging for Level-One products and services and giving away Level-Three value. Because they lack the tools and the processes to work consistently at Level Two *and* Level Three, they end up getting paid nothing for their best stuff! The

SunBridge method helps even experienced advisors provide recognizably greater value to their clients and donors, and they receive greater value in return.

The first step toward becoming a Level-Three advisor—understanding the Level-Three Endowment—is to recognize the value of client relationships based on Connection, Significance, Vision, Wisdom, and Trust. This requires first recognizing and understanding your clients' or donors' vision; then working to define and design how they want their business, family relationships, and the rest of their life to be; committing that vision to a set of written plans; and finally, helping to turn that blueprint into reality.

# establishing and maintaining level-two relationships

Level-Three advising presumes a close, trusting, long-term relationship with the client or donor, which is why a history with the client of Level-Two successes is prerequisite. And once a Level-Two relationship has been established, it must be maintained. Just as personal relationships need attention and communication to stay healthy and vital, professional Level-Two relationships need regular attention and care to stay strong.

The transition to Level Three evolves naturally for some clients; others need one or more invitations. During this time, the advisor must create opportunities to regularly reconnect with the client's issues of meaning, life-story, and heart. While maintaining the Level-One products or documents is necessary, it is not sufficient. A document-maintenance or product-maintenance program will not suffice; there must be a process to maintain the *relationship*.

# trying on level three

As always, by listening to each client's or donor's stories, you'll know if and when the timing is right for this next step into an even richer world of connection and value. Two of the most effective SunBridge tools for testing the client's or donor's readiness to move into Level Three and for strengthening the bond between the advisor and the client or donor are *The Personal Legacy Declaration* and *The Meaning of Success Priceless Conversation.*

# the personal legacy declaration

Because the client's life story provides the perfect framework for Level-Three assessment, I encourage my clients who seem ready to move into a Level-Three relationship to write a profile that captures their wisdom, values, and feelings about life. We call this a *Personal Legacy Declaration.* It's a professionally designed collection of questions based on the Life Circle and the Legacy Circle that guides the client or donor to the discovery of his or her own life story by jotting down key experiences, identifying enduring values, disclosing persistent themes, and so on. When completed and evaluated, such an instrument provides the advisor with a living snapshot of the client or donor that, quite remarkably, may give the advisor a better sense of who the client or donor is than even members of his or her family may have.

There are financial advisors and estate planners who ask their clients to complete questionnaires and surveys, but these are usually engineered to steer the client toward certain predetermined financial products or services, or as a way to keep the conversation going while the "real" business of financial or estate planning is worked out. The *Personal Legacy Declaration,* by contrast, *is* the real business; it goes to the heart of the process and informs, directs, and drives all subsequent decisions about how to serve the client or donor.

The *Personal Legacy Declaration* has its roots in many cultures. Most notable among them, perhaps, is Judaism's tradition of creating and leaving an "ethical will" for posterity. These documents contain practical wisdom and insights from the writer's life, often including aspirations for his or her descendants. Some are crafted in a beautiful, poetic style; others are written more simply, sometimes consisting of nothing more than a two-page letter. As my story about my mother shows, this can be more than enough. The power of such declarations is that they come from the heart, where all value is rooted. Words that come from the heart touch the heart.

Working from the heart in this way may be foreign to you, but we can tell you from consistent experience that the destination is well worth the journey. The important thing is to get started! "Time flies," as the saying has it, and too often we let years, decades, even our entire life go by without offering the best of us, our true wealth, to those we care about most.

You don't, however, need a formal document to get the process going. Another approach is simply to write a letter to someone you care about in which you complete one or more of the following phrases:

- Some of the important lessons I've learned are…
- My definition of true success is…
- The formative events of my life were…
- The people who had the most profound influence on me are…
- Scriptural passages that mean the most to me include…
- These are some of my most precious possessions. I want you to have them because…
- I want to ask your forgiveness for…
- You are important to me because…

Questions of this sort allow you to begin seeing the big picture of the client's past and present—essential information for mapping the client's ideal future.

If you've never written a letter to your loved ones telling them about the person you are—your dreams and accomplishments, your hopes and best vision for the future, the things that matter to you most, the lessons that you've learned and want to pass along—we encourage you to take the time to do it now. Nothing will give you a more direct and powerful sense of the usefulness of this tremendous tool for client service like experiencing it yourself.

And don't be intimidated by thinking that you have to write in a grand style. Many of us find the prospect of expressing intimate thoughts and feelings a bit daunting. Make a start anyway! Allowing ourselves to be visible in this way is far easier to do than to think about doing. It doesn't matter if the finished document is elegant or plain, short or long, philosophical or simple. It only matters that it's yours.

# the meaning of success priceless conversation

*The Meaning of Success Priceless Conversation* uses a different route than *The Personal Legacy Declaration*, but it arrives at the same destination: it gets to the heart of the process and informs, directs, and drives all subsequent decisions about how to serve the client or donor. It uses the client's or donor's own words, thoughts, insights, and stories to discover and clarify how the client or donor sees life, what he or she values in life, and what ultimately he or she wants from life.

Just as each one of us has developed our own unique definition of the meaning of money based on a collection of experiences called "meaning of money stories," we also have developed our own unique definition of what it means to be successful, again based on a set of experiences that we in SunBridge call "meaning of success stories." *The Meaning of Success Priceless Conversation* uses a set of story-leading questions and an interview to help the client or donor recall and share these stories, and then draw his or her own conclusions from them. From that interview, the Level-Three Advisor develops a clear understanding of what to offer the client or donor.

There are many facets of success in life; *The Meaning of Success Priceless Conversation* focuses on five of them:

- Professional success
- Success in learning and education
- Financial success
- Success in relationships
- Personal and spiritual success

Within each of these five areas of focus, clients or donors are invited to recall life experiences that helped to shape the way they define success. From these stories, they are invited to compare their early definitions of success in each area with their current views, and to identify secrets to success they have distilled from those experiences. When I am working with clients, I sometimes share this example of a learning-and-education "meaning of success story" from my own life.

> *As an elementary school student, getting good grades was always easy for me, so report card day was always a piece of cake. At least it was until fifth grade in Miss Ratliff's class.*
>
> *Miss Ratliff was a tall, awkward woman who wore professorial half-glasses, pulled-back-into-a-bun hair, and most of the time a severe, judgmental expression. She expected a great deal from her students. Fun and horseplay were never permitted in her class.*
>
> *Miss Ratliff employed, I discovered on the first report card day of the school year, her very own custom-designed report card, one I had never seen before and never since. Besides the usual places for letter grades for academic subjects and for "S's" and "U's" for deportment, at the bottom there were two statements and a place for Miss Ratliff to check one or the other. They read:*
>
> *"Student works to the best of his ability."*
>
> *"Student does not work to the best of his ability."*
>
> *When report cards were handed out that day, I scanned mine to confirm the usual complement of A's and S's, then carried it home to my parents. After supper, I went to my parents' room for my customary report-card-day meeting with my dad, fully expecting the usual commendation for another job well done. To my surprise, I found my father looking rather stern and displeased.*
>
> *"Scott, I'm concerned about your report card," he said.*
>
> *"But dad," I protested, "I got straight A's and straight S's. You can't get any better than that."*
>
> *"Maybe so," he replied, "but look down here at the bottom. It says you are not working to the best of your ability."*

*"Oh," I uttered and swallowed hard. My mind was racing. "Who does she think she is?" I thought to myself. "I'm her star pupil. It's not my fault that her work is too easy for me and that I can just coast to an easy A." But I didn't disagree with her assessment. My dad went on, cutting off my thoughts.*

*"Son, I'm happy that you got good marks, but I'm disappointed that you seem to think that going to school is just about getting a grade. It's not. It's about getting an education, and for someone with your capabilities, that means pushing yourself, reading ahead, exploring on your own, asking for extra credit assignments, being curious. For some people, straight A's are not good enough. Do you understand?"*

*I nodded my head, a little puzzled but starting to see a bigger perspective. "I think so, dad." I mumbled.*

*"Well, I hope that Miss Ratliff never has to check the 'does not work to the best of his ability' box again."*

*"Me too," I said, relieved to be getting off with just a warning. "Me too."*

*Happily I can report that she never did all the rest of fifth grade.*

That experience and many others, I tell my clients, helped to shape my sense of what it means to be successful in learning and education. Those experiences also helped me figure out some of the secrets to success, and gave me a sense of satisfaction for the achievements I enjoyed and a quest for further things I still had left to accomplish.

"Like you," I say to my clients, "I have similar experiences, similar definitions, similar secrets, and similar longings in the other areas of my life, financially, professionally, personally, spiritually, and in relationships. As your advisor, I want to understand how you define success. I want to capture your secrets to success in all facets of your life. I want to hear of your accomplishments, your moments of feeling proud of yourself.

"And most important of all, I want to know *what's still missing for you, what's still left to do or achieve or become, in order for you to feel completely successful in your life.*"

I love the structure and simplicity of The Meaning of Success Priceless Conversation, and the fact that when finished I can deliver a beautiful package for the client's or donor's legacy library. It makes it easy because the process, the experience, and the deliverable all come in one elegant kit.

But just as with the Personal Legacy Declaration, it is not imperative that you employ a formal process to begin to understand what's still missing for the client or donor, and to learn what the next steps need to be. In certain situations, I can achieve approximately the same result using three questions to lead into a thoughtful and meaningful discussion, especially if my listening skills are up to par. Those three questions are:

1)  If you had an abundance of time, energy, and money, how would you live your life?
2)  If your doctor told you that you had three years to live, what would you do with that time?
3)  If your doctor told you that you had 24 hours to live, what regrets would you have?

> **"Most important of all, I want to know what's still missing for you, what's still left in order for you to feel completely successful."**

Once again, questions of this sort, combined with transformational listening, allow you to begin seeing the big picture of the client's or donor's past and present—essential information for mapping their ideal future. From there, it's time to show the client or donor you have a process for accomplishing the three roles of the Level-Three Advisor: architect, drafter of blueprints, and general contractor.

# what's next? planning

Sometimes, clients and donors initiate the process. They approach you seeking assistance in accomplishing the next big thing they crave for their life, their marriage, their family, their business, their giving, or their legacy. At other times, the life-review aspects of *The Personal Legacy Declaration, The Meaning of Success Priceless Conversation,* or some similar process draw a compelling craving to the surface and make it clear to them they must do something about it right away.

I use a simple question in those situations to focus and clarify their urgency and to launch a Level-Three conversation: **"WHAT'S NEXT?"**

*Advisor:* "It's nice to hear from you, John. How have you been?"

*Client:* "Not well. I was in the hospital last week. They thought it may have been a stroke or a series of strokes, but they're not completely sure. However, it sure scared the willies out of me."

*Advisor:* "Oh no. That sounds serious. Tell me more."

*Client:* "I just don't know whether I'm going to be able to keep running our family business, and I realize I need to make sure Mark is firmly in charge. You've been telling us for years we need a transition strategy, and now I know we can't put it off any longer. I realize that if this stroke had been more serious, we'd have a real mess on our hands right now."

*Advisor:* "I can tell by the sound of your voice that this is vitally important to you. I want to help you and your family, and I think I can. But tell me as succinctly as you can, what's next? What's the next thing we need to do now?"

*Client:* "I need you to help me pass the reins over to Mark. I know we've been talking about this for years and I've been putting it off, but now it's time."

\* \* \*

*Advisor:* "*Mary, here's your Meaning of Success Priceless Conversation gift box, ready for you to add to your Legacy Library. That was such a delightful experience for me to share with you.*"

*Client:* "*Thanks so much. It really was enjoyable. But it got me thinking.*"

*Advisor:* "*About what?*"

*Client:* "*About the fact that I never finished college. We got married when Ted graduated and we always said I'd go back after we got settled, but then we started having babies, and things got so busy and it just never happened. Now that Ted is gone . . . .*"

*Advisor:* "*It sounds like you've got something in mind for your next big step? What is that?*"

*Client:* "*I want to go back to college and finish my degree. Imagine that, at my age! But I don't know where to even start. I guess I need someone to help me figure out how to do that. I trust you. Could you help me with that?*"

With the answer to the "What's next?" question clearly on the table, the advisor needs to follow four more steps:

1)    Ask: What makes this so important to you?
2)    Ask: What are the consequences if we don't take care of this?
3)    Ask: What are the benefits if we do take care of this?
4)    Describe: Here's my process for helping you addressing this issue.

The three questions help the client or donor and the advisor appreciate more fully why accomplishing the next step truly matters. By answering them candidly and thus developing and clarifying within the client's or donor's mind two sharply contrasting stories—the negative story of not reaching the desired objective and the positive story of doing so—the client or donor reinforces their internal drive to get going. It is the clarity and juxtaposition of these two internal narratives that drive the client or donor to action.

The description of your process tells the client or donor that you have a system for finding the best answers to their problems and delivering solutions. It also shows that you are experienced, that you understand people in their situation, that you are thoughtful and systematic, and that you can guide them to where they want to go. It gives them the confidence to follow you.

# strategic vision: putting it all together

At this point it's time to begin plotting a course for improving an aspect of the client's or donor's future, such as family relations, health, investments, and so on. We call this process the *Strategic Vision*. There are a number of SunBridge tools available for accomplishing this; for example, we use a variety of worksheets such as the *"Get It Done Action Plan"* or the *"Strategic Vision"* template. With a larger group, we may use a portable storyboard and colored Post-It® Notes. On these we write the client's or donor's best thinking on several important questions:

1) What aspect of your life do you want to change?
2) Why is it important for you to do so?
3) Where are you now?
4) What if you stay where you are now?
5) What might be holding you back from moving forward?
6) Where do you want to be a year from now? In the next 90 days?
7) What are the benefits of reaching those objectives?
8) What action steps are necessary for you to get from where you are now to where you want to be?

The result of the thinking process engendered by this series of questions is a set of clear and specific actions steps to be taken, some by the client or donor, some by the advisor, and some by other people.

A client's or donor's *Strategic Vision* or *Get It Done Action Plan* may include anything from losing ten pounds and rediscovering romance with a spouse to founding an international philanthropic organization. The only rule is: If it matters to the client or donor, it matters. We have seen that this *Strategic Vision* approach allows the client or donor to keep both broad vision and next-steps clear and present.

The advisor can then set up this set of action steps in a simple X-Y grid, with the various action items along one axis and relevant time intervals along the other. This graphing is what translates the vision from theory or ideal into practice, while the simplicity of the structure ensures that it stays flexible and therefore useful.

One of our colleagues who took the SunBridge training said that *Strategic Vision* takes the "airy-fairy" of a mere vision and turns it into the "nitty-gritty" of tangible steps needed for the realization of that vision. This is the essence of Level Three.

> **Strategic Vision takes the "airy-fairy" of a mere vision and turns it into the "nitty-gritty" of tangible steps needed for the realization of that vision. This is the essence of Level Three.**

It is not just about getting the big picture of the client's or donor's life, beyond the situational stories shared by the client at Level Two. It's about identifying the life story, the through-lines of concern, the abiding and persistent values and interests, and crafting them into a guidebook, a map, a tangible plan. Some of us may go our entire lives without finding someone willing and able to serve as an ally in this process. At Level Three, this is precisely what your clients or donors find in you.

Another Level-Three tool we use at SunBridge is a process called *The Story of the Rest of Your Life*. Here, the advisor leads the client through a series of questions that lend imaginary form to the life the client would like to be living five, ten, and twenty years hence. It's a great tool for exercising the muscles of imagination, and certainly can set the stage nicely for the more comprehensive and detailed *Strategic Vision* plan.

# turning vision into reality

As rewarding as it is for the client or donor and his advisor to envision the future of the client's or door's business, his family relationships, or his life through SunBridge tools such as *Strategic Vision, Get It Done Action Plan,* or *The Story of the Rest of Your Life,* stopping at that point would leave the real promise and potential of a Level-Three relationship unfulfilled. Defining and designing the vision is the beginning of the process, not the end. Once the blueprint has been created, it's time to start building.

At this stage, the Level-Three advisor is likely to serve as the general contractor under the client's or donor's direction. The advisor facilitates the many action steps worked out in the *Strategic Vision.* Many of these steps will fall within the range of the advisor's professional skills and knowledge, and he will render direct service to the client. Many more will lie outside the advisor's formal qualifications and training; in these cases he will coordinate with the client or donor to engage experts in those fields. Collaboration is a key skill at this stage of the process.

The Level-Three advisor is not—nor does he or she need to be—a psychologist, marriage counselor, family historian, travel agent, geriatric caregiver, or any other specialist than the one he or she already is. Such experts can be called upon as needed to give "legs" to the client's vision, so the mission of his or her life can be fulfilled. The Level-Three advisor helps the client or donor turn the vision into reality by discerning and facilitating the client's mission in life; he doesn't try to be a jack-of-all-trades.

Besides helping the client or donor engage other assistance as needed, the Level-Three advisor's real value in the implementation stage is to provide support, accountability, encouragement, counsel, training, monitoring, and constant updating and refinement of the *Strategic Vision.* The advisor also offers the client or donor perspective, balance, insight, and reality checks. The ultimate value to the client or donor is seeing steady progress toward the future world in which the client or donor wants to live. Our frequent experience is that Level-Three clients and donors recognize, appreciate, and pay well and willingly for this remarkable service.

Let's take a look at how Level-Three advising compares with Levels One and Two:

---

### Level Three: Mission

Connection, Significance, Vision, Insight & Wisdom,
Lifelong Value

### DISCERNMENT

### Level Two: Meaning

Relationships, Understanding, Context, Perspective & Dialogue,
Long-Term Solutions

### STORY

### Level One: Money

Transactions, Documents & Products, Formulas, Time & Advice,
Short-Term Answers

---

# level-three client and donor service

In the first chapter, we identified the cornerstones of a Level-One Practice. To review, they are:

**Method:** Mind
**Main Focus:** Money

**View of Client/Donor:** Balance Sheet
**Vision:** Quick-Fixes

At Level Two, you do what you've always done but in a different way; at Level Three, you do something wholly different. The core elements of Level-Two client or donor service, you may remember, are:

**Method:** Heart
**Main Focus:** Meaning
**View of Client/Donor:** Whole Person
**Vision:** Connection

Level Three expands these to a level of fulfillment and value that is, in principle, unlimited:

**Method:** Significance
**Main Focus:** Identity
**View of Client/Donor:** Force for Good
**Vision:** Living Legacy

## Significance

---

*"Few may touch the magic string, and Noisy Fame is proud to win them. Alas for those who never sing, but die with all their music in them."*
*—Oliver Wendell Holmes*

---

As a Level-Three advisor, you are no longer concerned primarily with transactions, as you are at Level One; or even with stories and connection, as you are at Level Two. The focus shifts at Level Three to *significance,* that vector of meaning that runs through a person's life.

[
**It's time to show the client or donor you have a process
for accomplishing the three roles of the Level-Three Advisor:
architect, drafter of blueprints, and general contractor.**
]

Significance emerges when there is a collaboration of mind and heart, a synthesis of the methods of Levels One and Two, following the idea that heart without mind can be mere sentiment, while mind without heart can be, well, heartless. As the advisor gains a sense of what the client's or donor's life has been, is and aims to be, he or she is in a unique position to serve as the client's or donor's standard-bearer, coach, and ally. The advisor does not assume this role *in loco parentis*—the client or donor is, of course, still responsible for the vision and its fulfillment.

But once the significance of a client's life has been identified and articulated, something remarkable happens to that life. The client's or donor's willingness, trust, and accountability, encouraged by the advisor, crystallize into concrete steps that lead directly to the realization of ideals that, for lack of vision, direction, or both, have remained unfulfilled in the client's or donor's experience thus far.

## Identity

---

*"Don't ask yourself what the world needs; ask yourself what makes you come alive. And then go and do that. Because what the world needs is people who have come alive." —Harold Whitman*

---

Level-Three advising takes place at the most fundamental level of a person's life: his or her identity. Through identifying significance, translating this significance into the *Strategic Vision*, and supporting the client or donor in taking and staying true to the steps needed to realize that vision, the advisor becomes something of a spiritual midwife who assists the client or donor in giving birth to a better, more fulfilled, and in the broadest sense, *wealthier* version of himself.

Actually, he's helping the client or donor to become more the self he always has been, but this paradox should in no way diminish the value of the service that the advisor provides. To the contrary, it's hard to imagine a greater service than supporting a person in becoming more fully who he or she is.

And as this process depends upon deep sympathies and connections between advisor and client or donor, it's safe to say that the process will have a profound effect on the identity of the advisor, as well. The Level-Three clients with whom I have worked have inspired, prompted, even compelled me to revise my sense of who I am—just as that client did who questioned my formulaic practices at Level One.

## Force for Good

*"Dream no small dreams for they have no power to move the hearts of men."* —
*Johann Wolfgang von Goethe*

As clients and donors gain greater clarity as to who they really are, they discover an increased desire to make a difference, to have a greater impact for good in their homes, their communities, and in the world. This pushes them to stretch themselves in service and generosity. They find new energy and new drive to reach out and touch the lives of others. Their creativity is spurred and their vision is expanded. They discover the joy of bigger thoughts, bigger dreams, and bigger results. And they discover that, once stretched, their souls can never again be satisfied with small ideas.

## Living Legacy

---

*"Fairy tales are more than true: not because they tell us that dragons exist, but because they tell us that dragons can be beaten."* — *G. K. Chesterton*

---

Level Three is about transforming significance, through vision, into a living legacy. We say "living" because it is not just about posterity, though to be sure, the significance of a person's life can and often has affected many generations to come. It is precisely because the meaning of our life, in the richest sense of realized vision, can survive us and remain a living force that benefits others that we call it a legacy. It is not, however, a legacy we have to die to begin giving. We can begin giving it now.

# the success-full family: a level-three model

When we are engaged by parents or grandparents to help them create a living legacy, we often use a template to help them envision some of the key elements for creating a rich, full family life lasting and flourishing for multiple generations. This can be a challenging endeavor. Many financially successful families end up with children and grandchildren who live empty, purposeless lives, awash with material affluence and pampering but devoid of meaningful challenges and lacking opportunities to learn the values that made the family successful in the first place.

We use the Success-Full Family™ image as a map to guide families on the journey to a rich and rewarding multi-generational legacy.

# The Success-Full™ Family

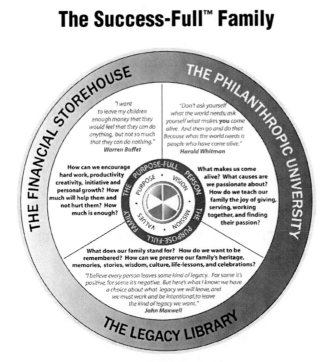

Transforming children and grandchildren often starts by reminding them—or in many cases, teaching them—about the family story. Without roots, trees topple over in strong winds and people are tossed to and fro when life gets tough, as it invariable does. Connecting or re-connecting children and grandchildren with who "their people" are and what they can learn from them provides an anchor of self-identity. Family history is a key piece of helping children of success lead full and purposeful lives.

The idea of using the portion of the family's financial resources that will pass to the heirs to encourage responsibility, growth, work, purposefulness, and family harmony in future generations, rather than to control, coddle, or emasculate them can be one of the most important new mind-sets we can introduce to the Level-Three families with whom we work.

The pioneering work of my good friend and colleague John A. Warnick is a wonderful example of this. John A. has created the break-through concept of Purposeful Trusts—wills, trusts and other legal documents that include the personal words of parents and grandparents to express the human (as contrasted with the purely legal) purposes behind planning and giving. When parents and grandparents envision and then re-imagine the way their wealth will actually be received by their children and grandchildren and how it will affect their lives, it creates an opportunity for advisors to touch hearts and change lives for generations to come.

> Level Three is about transforming significance, through vision, into a living legacy. It is not a legacy we have to die to begin giving. We can begin giving it now.

Perhaps the most immediately impactful component of the Success-Full Family model is The Philanthropic University. Many affluent families use some portion of their funds to support charitable causes, and we applaud that. However, some people limit their charitable giving because they fear that philanthropy might shortchange their own children and grandchildren. "Charity begins at home," they say.

We agree with the sentiment that helping our own kin is a significant priority, but we disagree with the notion that helping them means turning our back on charitable giving. Ironically, it turns out that the best way to bless the lives of children and grandchildren is by engaging multiple generations of the family in a common philanthropic enterprise. Such an approach can produce results far larger that "merely" feeding the hungry and saving the environment— it can literally transform the family for many generations.

A family philanthropic enterprise creates what most successful families in the past enjoyed—a collective activity like the family farm or ranch, a family business, or a religious mission—but which most families today do not have. It creates a shared purpose. It creates a common vision. It creates meaningful work for all.

A family philanthropic enterprise creates an opportunity to look beyond the family member's focus on self-gratification and see the needs of others. At the same time, it creates an environment in which the family's own needs can be addressed. It creates a common space, much like the tribal fire ring of old, where the wisdom of the elders can be shared and preserved, and the energy and creativity of the younger generations can be harnessed and given direction. It creates the ideal setting for teaching financial lessons, human insight, and family values.

In the Success-Full Family model, we encourage families of every level of financial wealth to set aside some of their money to endow their own Philanthropic University. The result of this "institution of higher education" is children and grandchildren who are caring, well-rounded, financially savvy, and more resistant to the ravaging infections of "affluenza." The result is parents and grandparents who have greater confidence in the future, as well as multigenerational families who know each other, love each other, and who can work together respectfully and harmoniously. It is the most effective process we have found for transforming families for good, while at the same time making a difference in the world.

# building bridges

In our workshops, we share a poem that captures something of the spirit of Level Three and the richness of the idea of a living legacy. The poem is entitled *The Bridge Builder*, by Will Allen Dromgoole:

> An old man going a lone highway
> Came at the evening, cold and gray,
> To a chasm, vast and wide and steep,
> With waters rolling cold and deep.
> The old man crossed in the twilight dim,
> That sullen stream had no fears for him;
> But he turned when safe on the other side,
> And built a bridge to span the tide.

"Old man," said a fellow pilgrim near,
"You are wasting your strength with building here.
Your journey will end with the ending day,
You never again will pass this way.
You've crossed the chasm, deep and wide,
Why build you this bridge at eventide?"

The builder lifted his old gray head.
"Good friend, in the path I have come," he said,
"There followeth after me today
A youth whose feet must pass this way.
This chasm that has been naught to me
To the fair-haired youth may a pitfall be.
He, too, must cross in the twilight dim—
Good friend, I am building the bridge for him."

The Level-Three journey, like all true journeys, is unpredictable—a process that brooks no formulaic answers. Advisor and client or donor must learn and discover as they go. This is precisely why there is no such thing as "instant Level-Three" advising. Level Three is a searching conversation between two friends who know each other well, and who, for the moment, are focusing on the unconditional and ultimate well-being of one of them. Within the arena of this conversation, miracles can and do happen. And there are no formulas for a miracle.

# marketing at level three

In marketing Level-Three services, you're dealing with a select audience: your Level-Two clients and donors. But the process should begin and the seed must be planted during the very first meeting, when you're telling the story of who you are and how you practice. At that moment, before the prospect has had a chance to pigeon-hole you as this kind of advisor or that, you must gently pull back the curtain a bit and let the client or donor know that, however he or she

> The beauty of the SunBridge model is its recognition of the value of each Level, and the respect for each client regardless of the level of service at which he or she chooses to operate.

chooses to work with you initially, there is the possibility of ultimately working together in a far grander fashion than he or she may have previously imagined.

Seldom will the client or donor understand or appreciate at that first meeting what this can mean; indeed, you should make it clear that even if he or she wanted to work with you at Level Three, it would not be possible immediately. But planting the seed early allows it to germinate and grow, and it is supremely beneficial to the client to be aware of this option even at the beginning.

As the relationship develops and matures, you may want to mention from time to time the level of service you offer that's designed to articulate a much farther reaching expression of the client's or donor's life story. As the client or donor becomes comfortable with this idea, you'll find that you can refer in natural and appropriate ways to Level Three, and even tell stories of the profound benefits you and your clients or donors have experienced working together in this way.

Because most prospects and clients are not aware of what a Level-Three relationship looks like and because it is, after all, a subtle and unexpected form of service, I've found it useful to share examples of *Strategic Vision* action plans and *The Story of the Rest of Your Life* profiles. Allowing clients to hold and turn the pages of these tangible embodiments of Level-Three work helps them to imagine themselves working with you as a Level-Three advisor.

Of course, the most important step in marketing at Level Three is creating and maintaining Level-Two relationships. Both you and your client or donor must experience real joy and value working with each other at Level Two; otherwise, there is no real possibility of moving on to a genuine Level-Three relationship. But if you do share and maintain authentic Level-Two relationships and have made your clients or donors aware that there is another level of service you offer, you'll find that, as if by magic, certain clients or donors will start to approach you about becoming their Level-Three advisor.

One of our "graduate school-level" SunBridge advisors recently shared with me an experience he'd had. Jerry had done some planning for a client off and on for a number of years, and the client had returned to Jerry for some additional services. In the course of working together, Jerry had created a wonderful Level-Two relationship with this client, focusing on the client's stories and issues of meaning, as well as the client's financial and legal concerns.

At an appropriate moment, Jerry described how he had begun working with select clients as a Level-Three advisor, explaining in general terms what this meant. One day, almost out of the blue, the client wanted to talk about Level Three. "I'm interested in exploring this idea further," he said. "Lately I've been re-evaluating the direction of my life, and have been imagining how great it would be to have someone to work with me in this, someone who already knows me well and has the tools to help me figure out where I want to go and how to get there. I feel like you know me so well from the way we've worked together, and I trust you and think you could help me sort things out. How do we get started?"

# epilogue:
# financial, legal and philanthropic consulting in an expanding universe

At the end of our lives and our clients' and donors' lives, we will each look back and ask ourselves three ultimate questions:

*Did I live?*
*Did I love?*
*Did I matter?*

This book has been written with the faith and hope that professional advisors of the caliber described herein can play a major role in determining how those questions get answered, both by advisors and by their clients and donors.

It has been written with the belief that the scope and thrust of our professional services can help clients and donors discover and honor those things that make them come alive; connect more deeply and meaningfully with family, friends, and community; and focus and intensify their impact in the world around them. It has been written with the further belief that when we as professional advisors make that our purpose and our mission, we inevitably and unavoidably produce the same results for ourselves.

We've traveled quite a way from the one-dimensional world of Flatland. Through the power of story, we expanded linear, transactional thinking into the three-dimensional world of Level Two, based on the view of the client as human being, and wealth as far more than money and property alone. Then, at Level Three, we expanded our view again—not in space but in time—taking into account the client's past, present and future in a *Strategic Vision* that translates the client's or donor's dreams into action steps.

We saw that, as financial, estate, and philanthropic advisors, we're actually in a position to provide the client and donor with a map to the best life he or she can envision, along with the direction, coaching, and support needed to see that he or she gets there. We saw that this expansion of time carries the arc of the client's or donor's life purpose into the future as legacy, with a beneficial influence that may continue from generation to generation without end.

We trust that none of this has left you with any feeling of prescription. It is not as though we should all be practicing at Level Three with all our clients, or even at Level Two. The beauty of the SunBridge model is its recognition of the value of each Level, and the respect for each client and donor regardless of the level of service at which he or she chooses to operate.

From the advisor's perspective, this flexibility is paramount, for several reasons. First, it allows you to meet the client where he or she is. Second, it allows you to offer increasingly sophisticated and valuable levels of service to those clients who want it, and even help them, through timely invitations, to become clear about the sort of professional relationship they want with you. In other words, it allows you to be flexible and responsive, and so, far more useful and valuable to the client. Finally, it gives you the opportunity to integrate your personal and professional life in a way that will fill you with an enthusiasm, passion, and purpose that we sometimes mistakenly think are reserved for the young.

SunBridge is different from the various "values-based" or "client-centered" programs out there. These programs invariably mask foregone conclusions that seek to maneuver the client into some predetermined "right answer," often involving either a certain type of investing or some form of charitable giving. They also presume that what they're offering can be applied to clients and donors across the board, in cookie-cutter fashion.

Nothing could be further from the reality of practice. Even at our Level Two, formulaic thinking is essentially passé, although our model provides useful guidelines. At Level Three, the advisor must be prepared to work without a net, to lead the client or donor by following, and to be surprised as both client/donor and advisor evolve through the process. At each level, service becomes less predictable but more valuable, justifying accordingly higher compensation. If, in order to avoid this unpredictability, an advisor tries to apply even the loftiest ideas as a formula, he or she will fail, because the client or donor isn't a formula.

This is a crucial difference between SunBridge and other models. It's not just that flexibility and the willingness to meet the client or donor at his or her level is a nice thing to do. Success depends on it. SunBridge not only shows you how to take a comprehensive, client-centered, values-based approach to service; it also shows you how to make a good living doing it.

It seems right and good to us that our success hangs on our willingness to recognize and serve our clients as whole people, recognizing their right to determine their level of service. Some clients may want to stay at Level One. Fine. We can accommodate. Others, hearing a story of ours, may respond with one of their own, perhaps a story that reveals something they care about greatly, and so something that can guide us in guiding them. And others, sensing deeper waters, may want to venture there to fulfill the story of their life in a way they had not previously imagined.

Our aim is to see that you have all the understanding, language, tools, concepts, and support you need to meet the client or donor at whatever depth he or she chooses. Flatland has its place, but we want you to be ready to offer more if more is wanted. We feel strongly that this sort of adaptability will continue to be a defining factor in the success of financial advisors, and in the not too distant future, will become the decisive one.

*This book is based on the SunBridge model. The principles and techniques it presents are identical to those we teach in the SunBridge Legacy Builder Retreat, the SunBridge Advanced Legacy Builder Retreat, and the Legacy Builder Network. If you have any questions or would like more information, please drop us a line at admin@sunbridgenetwork.com or visit us online at www.SunBridgeNetwork.com.*

# suggested reading

Arbinger Institute, *Leadership and Self-Deception*, San Francisco, CA; Berrett-Koehler Publishers, 2000.

Arbinger Institute, *The Anatomy of Peace*, San Francisco, CA; Berrett-Koehler Publishers, 2006.

Beckwith, Harry, *The Invisible Touch*, New York, NY; Warner Books, 2000.

Beckwith, Harry, *What Clients Love*, New York, NY; Warner Books, 2003.

Bradley, Susan, *Sudden Money*, New York, NY; John Wiley & Sons, 2000.

Buckingham, Marcus and Donald Clifton, *Now, Discover Your Strengths*, New York, NY; Free Press, 2001.

Buford, Bob, *Half Time*, Grand Rapids, MI; Zondervan, 1994.

Calloway, Joe, *Becoming a Category of One*, Hoboken, NJ; John Wiley & Sons, 2003.

Cochell, Perry and Rodney Zeeb, *Beating the Midas Curse*, West Linn, OR; Heritage Institute Press, 2005.

Clifton, Donald O. and Paula Nelson, *Soar with Your Strengths*, New York, NY; Delacorte Press, 1992.

Collier, Charles W., *Wealth in Families, Second Edition*, Cambridge, MA; Harvard University Press, 2008.

Covey, Stephen R., *Seven Habits of Highly Effective People*, New York, NY; Simon & Schuster, 1990.

Covey, Stephen R., *Seven Habits of Highly Effective Families*, New York, NY; Golden Books, 1997.

Covey, Stephen R., *The Eighth Habit*, New York, NY; Free Press, 2004.

Daniell, Mark and Sara Hamilton, *Family Legacy and Leadership*, Singapore; John Wiley & Sons, 2010.

Denning, Stephen, *The Springboard*, Boston, MA; Butterworth-Heinemann, 2001.

Denning, Stephen, *The Leader's Guide to Storytelling*, San Francisco, CA; Jossey-Bass, 2005.

Dungan, Nathan, *Prodigal Sons & Material Girls*, Hoboken, NJ; John Wiley & Sons, 2003.

Dunn, Paul and Ron Baker, *The Firm of the Future*, Hoboken, NJ; John Wiley & Sons, 2003.

Emmons, Robert A., *Thanks! How Practicing Gratitude Can Make You Happier*, New York, NY; Houghton Mifflin Publishers, 2007.

Farnsworth, Scott, *Double Your Sales: An Honest and Authentic Approach to Professional Selling*, Harmony, FL; SunBridge, 2009.

Farnsworth, Scott and Peggy Hoyt, *Like a Library Burning: Sharing and Saving a Lifetime of Stories*, Oviedo, FL; Legacy Planning Partners, 2008.

Fithian, Scott, *Values-Based Estate Planning*, New York, NY; John Wiley & Sons, 2000.

Gallo, Eileen and Jon Gallo, *Silver Spoon Kids*, New York, NY; McGraw Hill, 2002.

Gardner, Howard, *Changing Minds*, Boston, MA; Harvard Business School Press, 2006

Gary, Tracy, *Inspired Philanthropy, Third Edition*, San Francisco, CA; Jossey-Bass, 2008.

Gawain, Shakti, *Creating True Prosperity*, New York City, NY; MJF Books, 1997.

Gilmore, James H. and Joseph B. Pine, II, *Authenticity*, Boston, MA; Harvard Business School Press, 2007.

Gilmore, James H. and Joseph B. Pine, II, *The Experience Economy*, Boston, MA; Harvard Business School Press, 1999.

Goleman, Daniel, *Primal Leadership*, Boston, MA; Harvard Business School Press, 2002.

Greiff, Dr. Barrie Sanford, *Legacy: The Giving of Life's Greatest Treasures*, New York, NY; Regan Books, 1999.

Greene, Bob and D.C. Fulford, *To Our Children's Children*, New York, NY; Doubleday, 1993.

Heath, Chip and Dan Heath, *Made to Stick*, New York, NY; Random House, 2007.

Hughes, James E. Jr., *Family Wealth: Keeping it in the Family*, Princeton Junction, NJ; NetWrx, 1997.

Kim, W. Chan and Renee Mauborgne, *Blue Ocean Strategy*, Boston, MA; Harvard Business School Press, 2005.

Kline, Nancy, *More Time to Think*, Pool-in-Wharfedale, England; Fisher King Publishing, 2009.

Kline, Nancy, *Time To Think*, London; Cassell & Co., 1999.

LaSalle, Diana and Terry Britton, *Priceless: Turning Ordinary Products into Extraordinary Experiences*, Boston, MA; Harvard Business School Press, 2003.

Link, E.G. "Jay", *Family Wealth Counseling: Getting to the Heart of the Matter*, Franklin, IN; Professional Mentoring Program, 1999.

Lipman, Doug, *Improving Your Storytelling*, Little Rock, AR; August House Publishers, Inc., 1999.

Loehr, Jim and Tony Schwartz, *The Power of Full Engagement*, New York, NY; Free Press, 2003.

Maguire, Jack, *The Power of Personal Storytelling*, New York, NY; J.P. Tarcher/Putnam, 1998.

Maister, David, Charles Green, and Robert Galford, *The Trusted Advisor*, New York, NY; Free Press, 2000.

Markova, Dawna, *I Will Not Die an Unlived Life*, Berkeley, CA; Conari Press, 2000.

Maxwell, John C., *Thinking for a Change*, New York, NY; Warner Books, 2003.

McCarthy, Kevin, *The On-Purpose Business*, Colorado Springs, CO; Piñon Press, 1998.

McCarthy, Kevin, *The On-Purpose Person*, Colorado Springs, CO; Piñon Press, 1992.

Mitchell, Jack, *Hug Your Customers*, New York, NY; Hyperion Press, 2003.

Murray, Nick, *The New Financial Advisor*, Mattituck, NY; N. Murray Co., 2001.

Nomura, Catherine and Julia Waller, *Unique Ability*, Toronto, ON; The Strategic Coach, 2003.

Palmer, Parker J., *Let Your Life Speak*, San Francisco, CA; Jossey-Bass, 2000.

Reimer, Jack and Nathaniel Stampfer, *So That Your Values Live On*, Woodstock, VT; Jewish Lights Publishers, 1991.

Sheth, Jagdish and Andrew Sobel, *Clients for Life*, New York, NY; Fireside, 2000.

Snyder, Tom and Kevin Kearns, *Escaping the Price-Driven Sale*, New York, NY; McGraw Hill, 2008.

Stanley, Thomas J. and William D. Danko, *The Millionaire Next Door*, Atlanta, GA; Longstreet Press, 1996.

Stone, Richard, *The Healing Art of Storytelling; A Sacred Journey of Personal Discovery*, New York, NY; Hyperion, 1996.

Storycorps Project, *Listening is an Act of Love*, New York, NY; Penguin Books, 2007.

Taylor, Jill Bolte, *My Stroke of Insight*, New York, NY; Viking, 2008.

Warren, Rick, *The Purpose Driven Life*, Philadelphia, PA; Miniature Editions, 2003.

West, Scott and Mitch Anthony, *Storyselling for Financial Advisors*, Chicago, IL; Dearborn Financial Publishing, 2000.

West, Scott and Mitch Anthony, *Your Client's Story*, Chicago, IL; Dearborn Financial Publishing, 2005.

Wiersema, Fred, *Customer Intimacy*, Santa Monica, CA; Knowledge Exchange, 1996.

Williams, Roy and Vic Preisser, *Philanthropy, Heirs & Values*, Bandon, OR; Robert D. Reed Publishers, 2005.

Williams, Roy and Vic Preisser, *Preparing Heirs*, San Francisco, CA; Robert D. Reed Publishers, 2003.

Zeiler, Freddi, *A Kid's Guide to Giving*, Norwalk, CT; InnovativeKids, 2006.

# About The Author

**Scott Farnsworth** is an attorney and a Certified Financial Planner© who teaches financial, legal, and philanthropic professionals how to leverage the power of stories, the power of relationships, and the power of unique processes in their work with clients and donors. He is the president of SunBridge, Inc. and the founder of The SunBridge Legacy Builder Network.

Scott is a well-known national speaker and author. Besides this book, he is the author of *Like a Library Burning: Sharing and Saving a Lifetime of Stories;* and *Double Your Sales: An Honest and Authentic Approach to Professional Selling.* He has also served as Chair for the International Association of Advisors in Philanthropy National Conference.

In 2007, he was named one of *Financial Advisor Magazine's* "Innovators of the Year." He designs and delivers transformative workshops for professionals, including *"The Legacy Builder Retreat," "The Advanced Legacy Builder Retreat," "Mastering the High End Close," "The Double Your Sales Professional Workshop"* and *"The Wealth & Wisdom Summit."* He is the inventor of The SunBridge Money & Success Client Connection System ™, and is a certified Time to Think® Facilitator, Coach and Consultant.

Scott is a native of Fruitland, New Mexico. He earned his undergraduate degree *magna cum laude* in Portuguese and Political Science and his law degree *magna cum laude* at Brigham Young University. During law school he was the Managing Editor of the Law Review, and he published two scholarly articles. Following graduation, he was appointed Judicial Clerk for Paul H. Roney, Circuit Judge for the United States Court of Appeals for the Fifth Circuit.

In addition to his three decades of professional experience as an estate-planning attorney and financial planner, he was Vice President and Trust Officer at Trustmark National Bank and a professor of business law at the University of Southern Mississippi. He and his wife Marcie live in Harmony, Florida, and they have six children and six grandchildren.

To learn more, visit *www.SunBridgeNetwork.com.*

CPSIA information can be obtained at www.ICGtesting.com
Printed in the USA
LVOW091032290712

291844LV00001B/8/P